# Geographic
# Living-Cost
# Differentials

# Geographic Living-Cost Differentials

**Richard J. Cebula**
Emory University

**LexingtonBooks**
D.C. Heath and Company
Lexington, Massachusetts
Toronto

**Library of Congress Cataloging in Publication Data**

Cebula, Richard J.
  Geographic living-cost differentials.

  Includes index.
  1. Cost and standard of living—United States.
  2. United States—Economic conditions—1971-  —Regional disparities.  I. Title.
  HD6983.C36  1983      339.4′2′0973      82-48096
  ISBN 0-669-05968-4

*Copyright © 1983 by D.C. Heath and Company*

Published simultaneously in Canada

Printed in the United States of America

International Standard Book Number: 0-669-05968-4

Library of Congress Catalog Card Number: 82-48096

To David and Christy,
for their constant love

# Contents

# Figures

# Tables

# Preface and Acknowledgments

This book develops a systematic analytical and empirical approach to understanding the determinants of geographic living-cost differentials in the United States. By seeking to give insight into the causes of living-cost differentials, it endeavors to be not only of interest but also of great pragmatic value to both researchers and policymakers.

The book consists of four parts. The first part identifies the problem of geographic living-cost differentials in the United States. The second part develops a basic model of the determinants of living-cost differentials. The third part extends the model developed in the second part of the book. The fourth part of the book provides a summary and overview.

This project was undertaken over a period of three years (1980–1982). Over this time, several people have offered helpful suggestions or observations that have contributed to the project. Among these people, I especially wish to thank Milton Z. Kafoglis and Gordon Tullock. I also owe a debt of gratitude to my research assistants W. Lee Dawkins, Christy Cebula, and Michele Kaplan for their very competent, dependable, and gracious help. Finally, I wish to thank Micki Powell for her prompt, efficient, and gracious editorial and typing efforts.

# Part I
# Geographic Living-Cost Differentials in the United States

# 1

# Geographic Living-Cost Differentials in the United States: The Nature of the Problem

In this chapter, several major points are stressed. The most basic of these points is that there are enormous geographic living-cost differentials in the United States. The potential economic significance of these large geographic living-cost differentials is then discussed. Models of both individual and aggregate geographic mobility are constructed. In these models, the role of living-cost differentials in the rational migration decision is emphasized. The empirical findings of several earlier studies that investigated the impact of geographic living-cost differentials on mobility are then summarized, and the significance of the fact that living-cost differentials affect geographic mobility is discussed. It is stressed that internal migration in the United States is the single most important determinant of changes in the population distribution among geographic areas. Given that geographic differences in living costs profoundly influence regional labor markets and regional labor-market adjustments, it is noted that economic growth, tax rates, local public-goods provision, and wage rates are also very much affected by living-cost differentials among the different regions of the economy.

## The Existence of Great Geographic Living-Cost Differentials

The United States Bureau of Labor Statistics compiles geographically comparable data on living costs for three different living standards: low, intermediate, and high. In all three cases, the living-cost differentials among different regions of the economy are enormous (in relative terms). Based on survey data generated by the bureau for the autumn of 1981, the annual cost of maintaining a moderate standard of living for a typical family of four (consisting of a working husband, a nonworking wife, and two children) varies by as much as 41 percent from one geographic area to another. For example, in the four most expensive areas in the United States, the annual cost of maintaining a moderate standard of living in 1981 was $31,893 in Honolulu, Hawaii; $31,890 in Anchorage, Alaksa; $29,540 in New York City; and $29,213 in Boston, Massachusetts. By contrast, in the four least-expensive areas of the United States, the annual cost of maintaining a moderate living standing in 1981 was $22,678 in Dallas, Texas; $23,273 in

Atlanta, Georgia; $23,601 in Houston, Texas; and $24,498 in St. Louis, Missouri.

Data on the annual cost of maintaining a lower standard of living for a four-person family in 1981 reveal even greater geographic disparities (as much as 59 percent). For example, the annual cost of maintaining a lower standard of living in 1981 were highest in Anchorage, Alaska ($22,939), and Honolulu, Hawaii ($20,319); and lowest in Dallas, Texas ($14,392), and Atlanta, Georgia ($14,419).

A review of the Bureau of Labor Statistics data on the annual cost of maintaining a higher standard of living for a four-person family in 1981 also reveals major geographic disparities (as much as 49 percent). For example, the annual cost of maintaining a higher standard of living in 1981 ranged from highs of $50,317 in Honolulu, Hawaii, and $47,230 in New York City, to a low of $33,769 in Dallas, Texas.

It should also be observed that geographic living-cost differentials of essentially the same relative magnitude as those indicated in the examples have prevailed throughout the entire period (1966–1978) for which the Bureau of Labor Statistics has compiled such data.

Why do such enormous geographic living-cost differentials exist? Why do they persist (in relative terms) over time? What are the economic implications of these living-cost disparities? What are the various policy implications of these differential living-cost levels? This book addresses these questions. First, however, this chapter seeks to illuminate some of the potential economic significance of the existence of large geographic living-cost differentials.

## Economic Behavior and Money Illusion

The image of economic man requires that we view the individual as perfectly rational. The individual is portrayed as seeking to maximize utility subject to a budget constraint. Consider individual A, who has a utility function such as

$$U^A = U^A (X^A, Y^A) \qquad (1.1)$$

where

$U^A$ is an ordinal measure of individual A's utility;

$X^A$ is individual A's consumption of commodity X; and

$Y^A$ is individual A's consumption of commodity Y.

We may assume that the function in equation 1.1 is continuous and differentiable for all values of $X^A$, $Y^A > 0$. The budget constraint is given by

$$Px \cdot X^A + Py \cdot Y^A = I^A \qquad (1.2)$$

where

$Px$ is the unit price of commodity X;

$Py$ is the unit price of commodity Y; and

$I^A$ is individual A's money income.

As portrayed in equation 1.2, the individual is a price taker, that is, he as an individual exercises no control over the prices of either commodity X or commodity Y. The budget constraint that applies for an individual who has, for example, monopsony power over the price of commodity X, takes the following general form:

$$Px\,(X^A) \cdot X^A + Py \cdot Y^A = I^A \qquad (1.3)$$

Here, the price of commodity X to individual A depends on the amount of the commodity he purchases.[1]

In either case 1.2 or 1.3, rational economic behavior requries the individual to ascend the highest indifference curve attainable given his budget constraint. The budget constraint in turn is determined by the individual's money income and the vector of commodity prices.

Consumer-demand functions such as those that follow from equations 1.1 and 1.2 are homogeneous to degree zero with respect to money income *and* prices. Thus, a doubling of all prices and of money income would leave the consumer equilibrium unaltered. However, if a lower price for one or both commodities left the consumer decision unchanged, and hence the consumer's utility level unchanged, the individual in question would be subject to (and victim of) money illusion. Money illusion may be defined as the predication of economic decisions on *nominal* rather than *real* values. In what follows, it is assumed that the individual is entirely rational and is thus completely free of money illusion.

## A Model of Individual Economic Behavior in a Multiregional Context

Let the consumer now exist in an environment consisting of two regions, region B and region C. In either of these regions, the individual could derive utility from the consumption of the commodities available to him. In addition, in either of these two regions the individual could expect to receive a certain gross money income and to face a certain vector of commodity prices and a certain total tax liability.

Accordingly, in region B, individual A seeks to maximize a function such as

$$U^{AB} = U^{AB} (X^{AB}, Y^{AB}) \qquad (1.4)$$

subject to

$$DI^{AB} = I^{AB} - T^{AB} = Px^B \cdot X^{AB} + Py^B \cdot Y^{AB} \qquad (1.5)$$

where

$U^{AB}$ is individual A's utility level if living in region B;

$X^{AB}$ is individual A's consumption of commodity X if residing in region B;

$Y^{AB}$ is individual A's consumption of commodity Y if residing in region B;

$DI^{AB}$ is individual A's disposable money income if residing in region B;

$I^{AB}$ is individual A's gross money income if residing in region B;

$T^{AB}$ is individual A's total tax liability if residing in region B;

$Px^B$ is unit price of commodity X in region B; and

$Py^B$ is unit price of commodity Y in region B.

Similarly, in region C, the consumer seeks to maximize

$$U^{AC} = U^{AC} (V^{AC}, W^{AC}) \qquad (1.6)$$

subject to

$$DI^{AC} = I^{AC} - T^{AC} = P_v^C \cdot V^{AC} + P_w^C \cdot W^{AC} \qquad (1.7)$$

where

$U^{AC}$ is individual A's utility level if residing in region C;

$V^{AC}$ is individual A's consumption of commodity V if residing in region C;

$W^{AC}$ is individual A's consumption of commodity W if residing in region C;

$DI^{AC}$ is individual A's disposable money income if residing in region C;

$I^{AC}$ is individual A's gross money income if residing in region C;

$T^{AC}$ is individual A's total tax liability if residing in region C;

$P_v^C$ is the unit price of commodity V in region C; and

$P_w^C$ is the unit price of commodity W in region C.

Note that the commodity bundles *available* for the individual's consumption in regions B and C are not necessarily identical.

Refer now to figures 1–1 and 1–2. Figure 1–1 depicts consumer equilibrium for the individual in region B, whereas figure 1–2 depicts consumer equilibrium for the individual in region C. In figure 1–1, the individual maximizes utility subject to his budget constraint at point E, along indifference curve B'. In figure 1–2, the individual maximizes utility subject to his budget constraint at point F, along indifference curve C'. The decision of where the individual prefers to reside, that is, the individual's preference of

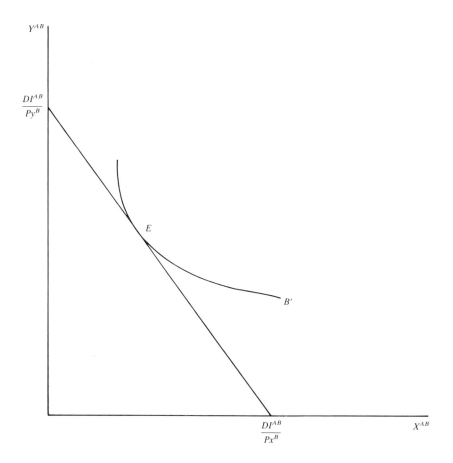

**Figure 1–1.** Maximum Utility in Region B

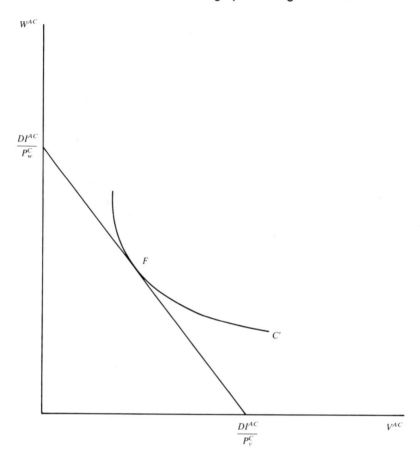

**Figure 1–2.** Maximum Utility in Region C

region B or C, is ultimately determined by the relative utility at points $E$ and $F$. If the individual's utility at point $E$ exceeds that at point $F$, he will prefer residence in area B. If the individual's utility at point $F$ exceeds that at point $E$, the individual will prefer to reside in area C.

   The choice of residence depends, among other things, on commodity prices as well as on disposable money income. A higher overall commodity-price structure in a region would tend, other things being equal, to discourage the individual from moving to that region.[2] Clearly, in a real-world context, large interregional living-cost differentials can be potentially very significant determinants of geographic mobility patterns.

   In this simple model of economic behavior, there is no allowance for geographic differentials in the levels of state-government and local-government tax burdens or provision of public goods and services. To allow for these two considerations, we must restructure the model.

Let us reconsider the two regions, B and C. In region B, let the individual seek now to maximize utility

$$U^{AB} = U^{AB} (X^{AB}, L^{AB}) \tag{1.8}$$

subject to

$$DI^{AB} = I^{AB} - T^{FAB} - T^{LAB} = Px^B \cdot X^{AB} \tag{1.9}$$

and

$$L^{AB} = L^{AB^*} \tag{1.10}$$

where

$U^{AB}$, $X^{AB}$, $DI^{AB}$, $I^{AB}$, and $Px^B$ are the same as earlier defined, and

$L^{AB}$ is the level of state plus local public goods and services available to individual A in region B[3];

$L^{AB^*}$ is a constant level of $L^{AB}$;

$T^{FAB}$ is individual A's federal tax liability in region B; and

$T^{LAB}$ is individual A's state plus local tax liability in region B.

In region C, the individual seeks to maximize

$$U^{AC} = U^{AC} (V^{AC}, L^{AC}) \tag{1.11}$$

subject to

$$DI^{AC} = I^{AC} - T^{FAC} - T^{LAC} = P_v^C \cdot V^{AC} \tag{1.12}$$

and

$$L^{AC} = L^{AC^*} \tag{1.13}$$

where

$U^{AC}$, $V^{AC}$, $DI^{AC}$, $I^{AC}$, and $P_v^C$ are as earlier defined, and

$L^{AC}$ is the level of state plus local public goods and services available to individual A in region C;[4]

$L^{AC^*}$ is a constant level of $L^{AC}$;

$T^{FAC}$ is individual A's federal tax liability in region C; and

$T^{LAC}$ is individual A's state plus local tax liability in region C.

The consumer (individual A) faces two linear constraints in both regions. In region B, the slope of his budget line is given by

$$dL^{AB}/dX^{AB} = -(Px^B/0).  \tag{1.14}$$

The slope of his budget line in region C is given by

$$dL^{AC}/dV^{AC} = -(P_v^C/0).  \tag{1.15}$$

The budget line in both cases is linear and perfectly vertical, that is, it has an undefined slope in both regions. In addition, in both regions the consumer faces a state-plus-local public-goods constraint. In region B, the slope of this constraint is given by

$$dL^{AB}/dX^{AB} = 0/L^{AB^*} = 0.  \tag{1.16}$$

In region C, the equivalent constraint is described by

$$dL^{AC}/dV^{AC} = 0/L^{AC^*} = 0.  \tag{1.17}$$

Refer now to figures 1–3 and 1–4. Figure 1–3, which represents region B to the individual, shows him to be in consumer equilibrium at point G, along indifference curve B*. Figure 1–4, which represents region C to the individual, shows him to be in consumer equilibrium at point H, along indifference curve C*. Once again, the consumer will choose to reside in the area that maximizes his utility. Thus, he will compare utility levels B* and C*. His final decision, as in the case of figures 1–1 and 1–2, will ultimately depend, among other things, on the magnitude of the differential living costs between the two regions. Once again, it may be surmised that if geographic living-cost differentials are relatively large, they may exercise a profound impact on geographic mobility.

## An Alternative Model of Individual Economic Behavior in a Multiregional Setting

The analysis developed in equations 1.1 through 1.17 assumes that the individual will predicate his location decisions on utility considerations.

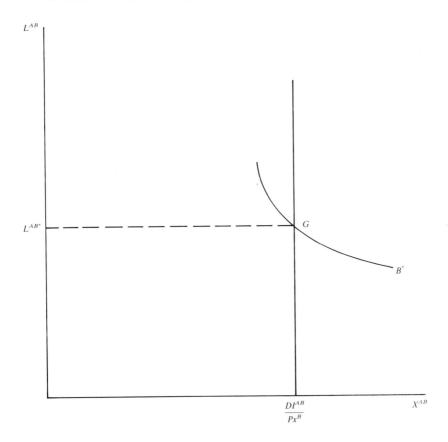

**Figure 1-3.** Maximum Utility in Region B, with Public Goods

Within this context, it was logically inferred that relatively large geographic living-cost differentials could potentially exercise a very significant impact on migration patterns. The same essential conclusion can be derived if we view the mobility calculus as an investment decision.

The notion that the decision to migrate is an investment decision can largely be traced to Sjaastad (1962) and Schultz (1961). Schultz (1961, p. 1), for example, has argued that "much of what we call consumption constitutes investment in human capital. Direct expenditures on . . . internal migration to take advantage of better . . . opportunities" is a clear example.[5] In this analysis, the investment in migration depends on two basic sets of forces: expected *real* income differentials, and expected differential benefits and costs from state- and local-government policies.

Once again, for simplicity, it is assumed that the economy consists of

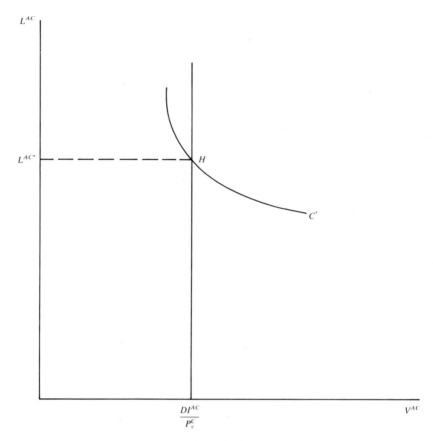

**Figure 1–4.** Maximum Utility in Region C, with Public Goods

two regions, region B and region C. It is also assumed that individual A currently resides in region B. Let $I^B_{At}$ be the money income expected in region B by individual A during year $t$, and let $I^C_{At}$ be the money income expected in region C by individual A during year $t$. The discounted present value of the expected nominal income differential between regions B and C for individual A, $D^{BC}_{IA}$, is given by

$$D^{BC}_{IA} = \sum_{t=1}^{n_A} (I^C_{At} - I^B_{At})(1 + i_A)^{-t} \qquad (1.18)$$

where $i_A$ is individual A's discount rate, and $n_A$ is individual A's time horizon.

Rather than arbitrarily assuming that all individuals have the same rate of discount, equation 1.18 ascribes a unique rate of discount to each individual. This procedure is based on the finding by Renas and Cebula (1972, p. 61) that "the marginal rate of time preference is a function of a person's socioeconomic status."

As noted in the discussion of equations 1.1 through 1.3, the absence of money illusion requires an individual to be concerned not only with his expected money income in regions B and C, but also with the levels of living costs in regions B and C. Let the expected *private* cost of living during year $t$ in regions B and C be represented by $M_{At}^B$ and $M_{At}^C$, respectively. Accordingly, the discounted present value for individual A of the expected living-cost differential between regions B and C, $(D_{MA}^{BC})$ is given by

$$D_{MA}^{BC} = \sum_{t=1}^{n_A} (M_{At}^C - M_{At}^B)(1 + i_A)^{-t}. \qquad (1.19)$$

The definition of private living costs in equation 1.19 is meant to exclude all direct costs associated with public policy per se.[6]

Combining the considerations in equations 1.18 and 1.19 yields the discounted present value for individual A of the expected *real* income differential between regions B and C, $D_{(I/M)A}^{BC}$:

$$D_{(I/M)A}^{BC} = \sum_{t=1}^{n_A} (I_{At/M_{At}^C}^C - I_{At/M_{At}^B}^B)(1 + i_A)^{-t}. \qquad (1.20)$$

As the analysis of equations 1.8 through 1.17 indicates, the state- and local-government policies in regions B and C potentially enter as arguments in the individual's migration decision. In order to allow for such public policies in the migration-decision process, we let the expected real value to individual A during year $t$ of all state- plus local-government public goods and services in regions B and C be $L_{At}^B$ and $L_{At}^C$, respectively. In addition, we let the real value to individual A during year $t$ of the expected state- plus local-government tax liabilities in regions B and C be $T_{At}^B$ and $T_{At}^C$, respectively. The discounted present value of the differential expected real net benefits from state and local government, $D_{GA}^{BC}$, is given by

$$D_{GA}^{BC} = \sum_{t=1}^{n_A} [(L_{At}^C - T_{At}^C) - (L_{At}^B - T_{At}^B)](1 + i_A)^{-t}. \qquad (1.21)$$

The quantities $(L_{At}^C - T_{At}^C)$ and $(L_{At}^B - T_{At}^B)$ represent the values of the expected fiscal surpluses in regions C and B during year $t$.[7]

Synthesizing equations 1.20 and 1.21 logically yields the total discounted present value of all the expected real net benefits to individual A of moving from region B to region C, $D_A^{BC}$:

$$D_A^{BC} = \sum_{t=1}^{n_A} [(I_{At/M_{At}^C}^C - I_{At/M_{At}^B}^B) + (L_{AT}^C - T_{AT}^C - L_{At}^B + T_{At}^B)](1 + i_A)^{-t}.$$

(1.22)

The results of equation 1.22, in which the migration decision is treated as an investment decision, indicate that geographic living-cost differentials can potentially exercise an immense influence over an individual's geographic mobility. This analysis is entirely compatible with those of the systems shown by equations 1.4 through 1.7 and 1.8 through 1.17.[8]

### A Model of Aggregate Migration and the Cost of Living

The models analyzed thus far have all been models of *individual* economic behavior; the stress has been on how the location decisions of *individuals* may be significantly influenced by geographic living-cost differentials. In this section, we develop a model of *aggregate* migration, a model that prepares us for the empirical discussion and analysis in the subsequent sections of this chapter.

The economy is again assumed to consist of two regions, region B and region C. In each of these two regions, the firms (employers) are assumed to employ a single, perfectly homogeneous labor input, which is purchased under perfectly competitive labor-market conditions.[9] All labor-demand curves are shown below as negatively sloped with respect to the the money-wage rate.

The *short-run supply curve of labor* in a region is defined as the number of units of labor forthcoming from *within* the region in response to changes in that region's wage rate. The short-run labor-supply curve does *not* allow for interregional migration.

The *long-run supply curve of labor,* for the purposes of this chapter, allows for geographic labor mobility between regions B and C in response to interregional wage-rate differentials.

Let the short-run supply function of labor in region B be represented by

$$N^B = N^B (W^B, P^B)$$

(1.23)

where

$N^B$ is the number of labor units supplied in region B from within region B;

$W^B$ is the money-wage rate in region B; and

$P^B$ is a measure of the average cost of living for a family unit in region B.

Assuming the absence of money illusion, conventional economic theory argues that

$$\partial N^B/\partial W^B > 0, \ \partial N^B/\partial P^B < 0. \tag{1.24}$$

The short-run labor-supply function in region C is given as

$$N^C = N^C \ (W^C, \ P^C) \tag{1.25}$$

where

$N^C$ is the number of units of labor supplied in region C from within region C;

$W^C$ is the money-wage rate in region C; and

$P^C$ is a measure of the average cost of living for a family unit in region C.

Assuming the absence of money illusion, conventional economic theory argues that

$$\partial N^C/\partial W^C > 0, \ \partial N^C/\partial P^C < 0. \tag{1.26}$$

In the absence of private direct-moving costs,[10] the long-run labor-supply function in region B is given by

$$N^{LB} = N^{LB} \ (W^B, \ P^B, \ W^C, \ P^C) \tag{1.27}$$

where $N_{LB}$ equals the total number of units of labor supplied to region B and $W^B$, $P^B$, $W^C$, and $P^C$ are the same as for equation 1.25.

The restrictions imposed upon the partial derivatives in equation 1.27 are given by

$$\partial N^{LB}/\partial W^B > 0, \ \partial N^{LB}/\partial P^B < 0, \ \partial N^{LB}/\partial W^C < 0, \ \text{and} \ \partial N^{LB}/\partial P^C > 0. \tag{1.28}$$

The long-run labor-supply function in region C is given as

$$N^{LC} = N^{LC} \ (W^C, \ P^C, \ W^B, \ P^B) \tag{1.29}$$

where $N^{LC}$ equals the total number of units of labor supplied to region C and $W^C$, $P^C$, $W^B$, and $P^B$ are the same as in equation 1.25.

The restrictions imposed upon the partial derivatives in equation 1.29 are as follows:

$$\partial N^{LC}/\partial W^C > 0, \ \partial N^{LC}/\partial P^C < 0, \ \partial N^{LC}/\partial W^B < 0, \ \text{and} \ \partial N^{LC}/\partial P^B > 0. \tag{1.30}$$

Refer now to figures 1–5 and 1–6, where the labor markets for regions B and C, respectively, are represented. In both diagrams, all labor-demand schedules are negatively sloped, and all short-run labor-supply curves are positively sloped. The labor markets in regions B and C are initially shown to be simultaneously in full equilibrium at points $a$ and $b$, respectively, in

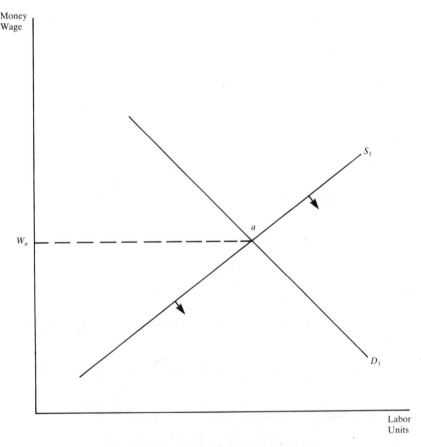

**Figure 1–5.** Labor Market in Region B

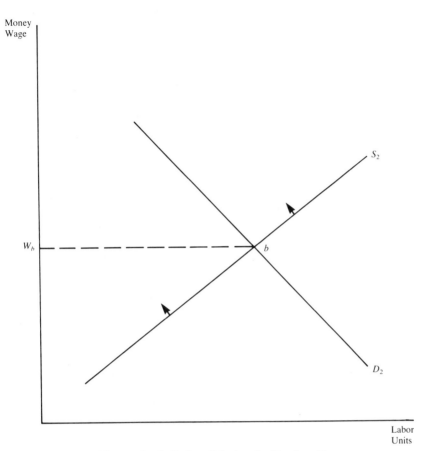

**Figure 1–6.** Labor Market in Region C

figures 1–5 and 1–6. Point *a* in figure 1–5 is at the intersection of labor-demand schedule $D_1$ and short-run labor-supply schedule $S_1$. Point *b* in figure 1–6 is at the intersection of labor-demand schedule $D_2$ and short-run labor-supply schedule $S_2$. As shown here, the equilibrium money-wage rate in region B is initially $W_a$, and the equilibrium money-wage rate in region C is initially $W_b$. For simplicity, we first let $W_a = W_b$.

Let us now assume that the cost of living in area C is higher than that in area B. Let us also assume that the residents of both regions have full information regarding the prevailing money-wage rates and living-cost levels in both regions. Thus, all labor units in regions B and C are aware of the existence of an interregional living-cost differential and aware of the magnitude of the differential.

Under the circumstances outlined in the preceding paragraph, it may be logically inferred that residents in region B (where the cost of living is lower) will not be willing to migrate to region C unless there is a money-wage-rate differential of sufficient magnitude to at least fully compensate them for the higher living-cost level in region C. By the same reasoning, it may logically be inferred that despite the equality of the initial money-wage rates in regions B and C ($W_a = W_b$), residents of region C would be willing to migrate to region B because they could raise their real wage-rate level.

This geographic migration can now be illustrated with the use of figures 1–5 and 1–6. Refer to points $a$ and $b$ in figures 1–5 and 1–6 respectively. A higher cost of living in region C induces a flow of migrants from region C to region B. This results in a leftward shifting of the short-run labor-supply curve in region C and a rightward shifting of the short-run labor-supply curve in region B. This shifting process is represented in figures 1–5 and 1–6 by arrows. The flow of migrants out of region C into region B will continue until there are no perceived net benefits from further migration. The latter condition will prevail only under the following condition:

$$W^B/P^B = W^C/P^C. \qquad (1.31)$$

The condition represented in equation 1.31 implies that, in full equilibrium in this model, the following obtains:

$$W^B/W^C = P^B/P^C. \qquad (1.32)$$

Thus, in full equilibrium, the ratio of money-wage rates must equal the ratio of living-cost levels. Clearly, an interregional living-cost differential implies an interregional money-wage-rate differential.[11] Perhaps even more importantly, an interregional living-cost differential acts to generate geographic mobility and thus to generate regional factor (labor-market) changes.

We may now generalize the analysis of equations 1.23 through 1.32 to include other considerations, adopting the same notation used in the analysis of equations 1.18 through 1.22. Based on these latter five equations, we may hypothesize that

$$P_A^{BC} = P_A^{BC} (D_A^{BC}) = P_A^{BC} (I_{Ab}^C, I_{Ab}^B, M_{Ab}^C, M_{Ab}^B, L_{Ab}^C, L_{Ab}^B, T_{Ab}^C, T_{Ab}^B, i_A) \qquad (1.33)$$

where $P_A^{BC}$ is the probability that individual A will migrate from region B to region C.

If we now expand equation 1.33 to include individual A's real direct out-of-pocket moving costs from region B to region C, $H_A^{BC}$, and individual A's foregone real earnings while in transit between region B and C, $E_A^{BC}$, we obtain the following equation.

$$P_A^{BC} = P_A^{BC} \, (I_{At}^C, \, I_{At}^B, \, M_{At}^C, \, M_{At}^B, \, L_{At}^C, \, L_{At}^B, \, T_{At}^C, \, T_{At}^B, \, i_A, \, H_A^{BC}, \, E_A^{BC},)$$

$$(1.34)$$

Let us now assume that, for simplicity, all persons residing in region B have homogeneous preferences.[12] We may then argue that the actual *aggregate* flow of migrants from region B to region C, $F^{BC}$, is given by

$$F^{BC} = P_A^{BC} \cdot V \qquad (1.35)$$

where $V$ is the total population in area B.

Substitution from equation 1.34 into equation 1.35 yields

$$F^{BC} = V \cdot P_A^{BC} \, (I_{At}^C, \, I_{At}^B, \, M_{At}^C, \, M_{At}^B, \, L_{At}^C, \, L_{At}^B, \, T_{At}^C, \, T_{At}^B, \, i_A, \, H_A^{BC}, \, E_A^{BC}).$$

$$(1.36)$$

Division of both sides of equation 1.36 by $V$ yields

$$F^{BC}/V = P_A^{BC} \, (I_{At}^C, \, I_{At}^B, \, M_{At}^C, \, M_{At}^B, \, L_{At}^C, \, L_{At}^B, \, T_{At}^C, \, T_{At}^B, \, i_A, \, H_A^{BC}, \, E_A^{BC}).$$

$$(1.37)$$

Equation 1.37 can easily be expanded to involve more than two re-gions.[13] In addition, equation 1.37 can be modified to allow for nonhomo-geneous preferences. Moreover, this model can be further modified to measure net rather than gross (one-way) migration flows. Thus, equation 1.37 can, in principle, be used to structure a regression model.

On the basis of the models of individual and aggregate mobility shown thus far in this chapter, it is clear that *in theory* geographic living-cost differentials may profoundly influence geographic mobility and regional labor-market adjustments. Next we will examine empirical evidence to determine whether *in fact* geographic living-cost levels influence migration (and hence labor markets).

## Geographic Living-Cost Differentials and Geographic Mobility: Previous Empirical Studies

Although the literature on the impact of geographic living-cost differentials on geographic mobility is relatively small, the conclusions reached by the studies involved are remarkably consistent and rather convincing.

The first rigorous study to examine empirically the potential impact of geographic living-cost differentials on migration was by Rabianski (1971). In this study Rabianski chose to use price indexes to deflate nominal earnings into real earnings. Dealing with a model of 1955–1960 gross aggregate migration patterns among some eleven Standard Metropolitan Statistical Areas (SMSAs), Rabianski compared the results of two migration regressions estimated by ordinary least squares. One regression included nominal earnings per capita as well as certain other explanatory variables; the second regression differed from the first solely by its inclusion of real rather than nominal earnings per capita. An examination of the two sets of regression results led Rabianski (1971, pp. 191–192) to conclude that

> in both models the T-ratios for the earnings ratios are significantly different from zero at the .01 level. . . . However, the inclusion of the inter-regional cost-of-living deflator did not significantly improve the models based upon nominal earnings.

In other words, Rabianski effectively found geographic living-cost differentials exercised no significant impact on geographic mobility patterns.

After several years of near-total neglect, the issue of geographic living-cost differentials and their impact on migration patterns surfaced again in 1978. Renas and Kumar (1978) deal with the determinants of aggregate net in-migration rates to SMSAs in the period 1960–1970. Their model hypothesizes that net in-migration is a function of: 1) median family income, 2) the cost of living, 3) the rate of change of median family income, 4) the rate of change of the cost of living, 5) the unemployment rate, and 6) selected quality-of-life variables.

Unlike Rabianski (1971), Renas and Kumar (1978) treat the cost of living as a separate independent variable. Renas and Kumar empirically estimate three alternative specifications of their basic model. The ordinary least-squares results indicate that the cost of living has a highly significant impact on net in-migration rates. As Renas and Kumar (1978, p. 101) observe, it "would thus appear that individuals do consider cost of living differentials among areas in formulating migration decisions."

This study by Renas and Kumar has received criticism and attention from a number of authors, most notably Alperovich (1979) and Cebula (1981). Alperovich criticizes the Renas and Kumar (1978) study for using a separate living-cost variable rather than using living costs to deflate nominal-income terms into real-income values. In their response to Alperovich (1979), Renas and Kumar (1979) examine two types of regression models, one with a separate living-cost variable and one with living costs used to deflate money income into real terms. Both models yield significant empirical results, leading again to the conclusion that geographic living-cost differentials do appear to influence geographic mobility patterns. Cebula's criticism of Renas and Kumar involves their failure to disaggregate migration flows by age group to allow for the effects of variations in the labor-force participation rate among different age categories of the population. In response to this commentary, Renas and Kumar (1981) examine empirically the determinants of net in-migration for twelve different age groups in the population between 1960 and 1970. Once again, Renas and Kumar (1981) find that living costs significantly affect migration flows.

In a study by Cebula (1979), the migration impact of geographic living-cost differentials is investigated through a variety of regression models. In the most developed of these models, Cebula (1979, pp. 82–87) hypothesizes the net in-migration rate to SMSAs to be a function of 1) medium income, 2) the rate of change of median income, 3) the cost of living, 4) the unemployment rate, 5) the median education level of the population, and 6) two separate dummy variables that reflect the quality of life. This model is estimated by ordinary least squares. Of the seven coefficients generated, six (including the cost of living) are found to be statistically significant at the 0.01 level or beyond. As in the studies by Renas and Kumar (1978, 1979, and 1981), Cebula (1979) finds the cost of living to exercise a profound impact on interregional migration patterns in the United States.

## New Empirical Evidence on the Impact of Living-Cost Differentials on Migration

The empirical model that follows examines geographic mobility for the period 1970–1978 and investigates the impact on migration of a number of economic and noneconomic variables in addition to the cost of living. The empirical results presented yield conclusions that are very similar to most of the studies just surveyed.

In order to investigate the impact of living-cost differentials on migration, the following model of net in-migration is hypothesized:

$$Ni = Ni\ (Ii,\ Ci,\ Qi,\ Ui) \tag{1.38}$$

where

$Ni$ is the net in-migration to region $i$;

$Ii$ is a measure of income levels prevailing in region $i$;

$Ci$ is a measure of living-cost levels in region $i$;

$Qi$ is a measure of the quality of life in region $i$; and

$Ui$ is a measure of unemployment in region $i$.

In accord with the results obtained in Cebula and Vedder (1973), Graves (1976), Greenwood (1969), Jones and Zannaras (1976), Kau and

Sirmans (1976), Liu (1975), Miller (1973), Renas and Kumar (1978), and
Vedder and Cooper (1974), the following restrictions are imposed on the
partial derivatives in equation 1.38.

$$\partial Ni/\partial Ii > 0, \ \partial Ni/\partial Ci < 0, \ \partial Ni/\partial Qi > 0, \ \partial N/\partial Ui < 0 \qquad (1.39)$$

Based on the model in equation 1.38, the actual regression to be
estimated is given by

$$Ni = a + bIi + cCi + dQi + eUi + \mu \qquad\qquad (1.40)$$

where

> $Ni$ is aggregate net in-migration to SMSA $i$, 1970–1978;
>
> $a$ is a constant term;
>
> $Ii$ is the 1969 median income level in SMSA $i$;
>
> $Ci$ is the 1970 cost of living in SMSA $i$ for a four-person family living on
> an intermediate urban budget;
>
> $Qi$ is a dummy variable indicating whether SMSA $i$ is located in a
> western state; $Qi = 1$ if the SMSA is located in a western state, and
> $Qi = 0$ otherwise;[14]
>
> $Ui$ is the 1969 unemployment in SMSA $i$; and
>
> $\mu$ is a stochastic-error term.

According to the hypothesized signs in 1.39, it logically follows that

$$b > 0, \ c < 0, \ d > 0, \ e < 0. \qquad\qquad (1.41)$$

There were sufficient data to estimate equation 1.40 for some thirty-six
SMSAs: Atlanta, Ga.; Austin, Tex.; Bakersfield, Cal.; Baltimore, Md.;
Baton Rouge, La.; Boston, Mass.; Buffalo, N.Y.; Chicago, Ill.; Cincinnati,
Ohio; Cleveland, Ohio; Dallas, Tex.; Dayton, Ohio; Denver, Col.; Detroit,
Mich.; Durham, N.C.; Hartford, Conn.; Honolulu, Hawaii; Houston, Tex.;
Indianapolis, Ind.; Kansas City, Mo.; Lancaster, Pa.; Los Angeles–Long
Beach, Cal.; Milwaukee, Wis.; Minneapolis–St. Paul, Minn.; Nashville,
Tenn.; New York, N.Y.; Orlando, Fla.; Philedelphia, Pa.; Pittsburgh, Pa.;
Portland, Maine; St. Louis, Mo.; San Diego, Cal.; San Francisco–Oakland,
Cal.; Seattle, Wash.; Washington, D.C. and Wichita, Kans.

The ordinary least-squares estimate of 1.40 yields

$$Ni = 660.2161 + 0.0399Ii - 0.0955Ci$$
$$\phantom{Ni = 660.2161 + }(+1.74)\qquad(-3.06)$$

$$+ 157.4934Qi - 3.6187Ui$$
$$(+3.45)\qquad(-9.51)$$

$$DF = 36 \qquad R^2 = 0.82 \qquad \langle R \rangle_{av}^2 = 0.79$$

$$F = \text{statistic} = 34.15 \qquad\qquad\qquad (1.42)$$

where terms in parentheses are $t$-values.

In the above regression estimate, the coefficients for all four independent variables have the expected signs. In addition, one coefficient is statistically significant at about the 0.05 level, whereas the other three coefficients are statistically significant at beyond the 0.01 level. The coefficient of determination and the adjusted coefficient of determination both have values in the range of 0.80, so that the model explains roughly four-fifths of the variation in the dependent variable. Finally, the $F$-statistic is statistically significant at well beyond the 0.01 level.

Overall, the regression results shown in equation 1.42 are very strong. Of greatest relevance in the equation is the result for the living-cost variable, $Ci$. The coefficient on $Ci$ is negative and statistically significant beyond the 0.01 level. This relationship is represented graphically in figure 1–7. We may infer that the results obtained here for relatively recent migration patterns (1970–1978) are entirely consistent with those obtained for the earlier period of 1960–1970 by Renas and Kumar (1978, 1979, and 1981) and Cebula (1979).

## The Significance of Geographic Living-Cost Differentials in the United States

Considerable evidence has been provided to indicate that in the United States geographic living-cost differentials do have a very significant impact on internal migration patterns. This section of the chapter delves into potential economic and public-policy implications of this influence of living costs on migration.

As West, Hamilton, and Loomis (1976) have observed, the U.S. Commission on Population Growth and the American Future, in *Population and the American Future,* Washington, D.C., U.S. Government Printing Office, Vol. 5, 1972 has focused attention on population distribution within the

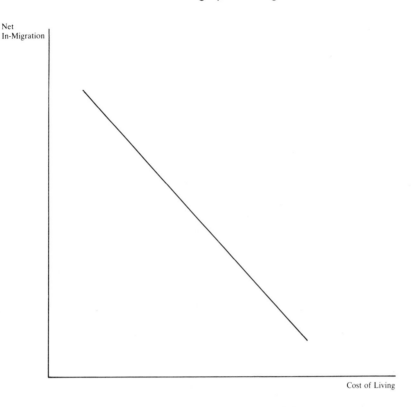

**Figure 1–7.** Migration and Living Costs

United States as a major national policy issue and concern. In this country, both birthrates and death rates have become comparatively stable. As a result, internal migration has become the principal short-run determinant of changes in population distribution and one of the principal long-run determinants of changes in population distribution.

Since geographic living-cost differentials exercise a significant influence on migration patterns, we may infer that living-cost differentials significantly affect the functioning of regional labor markets. By influencing regional labor markets, living-cost differentials affect the level and growth rate over time of money-wage rates; the level and trend over time of real-wage rates; and regional employment levels and trends. Living-cost differentials can profoundly influence regional economic growth rates by influencing the geographic distribution of labor (and the families thereof). In fact, because the most geographically mobile persons tend to be those possessing the greatest relative endowments of human capital, living-cost differentials could significantly contribute to a pattern of increasingly divergent regional growth rates in this country. Those regions possessing the lowest living-cost levels could easily become the beneficiaries of an immense long-term economic growth surge.

The influence of geographic living-cost differentials on migration may also generate a myriad of public-policy implications. For instance, an area with relatively low living costs may attract an influx of migrants. This would recreate a rising demand for local public goods and services in the area. It would also likely generate the need for new revenue or for increasing issues of tax-free bonds to finance capital improvements. The latter obviously would affect credit markets. Areas with relatively high living costs, in contrast, are likely to lose population and potentially be faced with a declining tax base and an unwanted excess capacity in the utilization of public capital.[15]

Because of the economic, social, and political ramifications of the influence of living costs on geographic mobility, insights about the determinants of geographic living-costs differentials may be useful to researchers, public-policy makers, businesses, and households. Providing such insights is the principal objective of the remaining chapters.

## Notes

1. In equation 1.2, the budget constraint is linear, and the slope is given by $dY/dX = -(Px/Py) < 0$. In equation 1.3, however, the budget curve is nonlinear and the slope is given by $dY/dX = -(1/Py) [Px^1 (X) \cdot X + Px(X)] < 0$. Since the budget line for equation 1.2 is linear and since the budget curve for equation 1.3 is concave to the origin, a unique consumer equilibrium is guaranteed in both cases so long as the indifference curves are of the usual form, that is, convex to the origin, continuous, and differentiable.

2. The computation of the price-structure differentials between the regions is obviously complicated by the probable nonhomogeneity of the commodity bundles available in the different regions.

3. The level of $L^{AB}$ is a constant for the individual, that is, he cannot influence—as an individual—the value of $L^{AB}$. This is mathematically shown in equation 1.10.

4. The level of $L^{AC}$ is a constant to the individual for the same reason that $L^{AB}$ is a constant to the individual. This is represented mathematically in equation 1.13.

5. Other analyses that treat migration as an investment decision include Bowles (1970), Gallaway and Cebula (1972), and Riew (1973).

6. Exclusions involve such considerations as property taxes, sales taxes, and nonfederal income taxes.

7. On the topic of the fiscal surplus, see Buchanan (1950).

8. This analysis ignores direct private costs of moving. As Sjaastad (1962, p. 81) observes, the "private costs (of moving) can be broken down into money and non-money costs. The former include the out-of-pocket expenses of movement, while the latter include foregone earnings and the 'psychic' costs of changing one's environment." Omitting such costs from the model does not alter our basic conclusions regarding the potential impact of living-cost differentials on geographic mobility.

9. It follows that all employers in both regions view labor units from both regions to be perfect substitutes for one another in the production process.

10. See footnote number eight.

11. Note that this money-wage rate differential exists *in equilibrium*.

12. This assumption is for mathematical convenience, not of any necessity.

13. For a good example of such an expansion (although living costs are omitted from the study), see Cebula, Kohn, and Vedder (1973).

14. Related to this dummy variable see Cebula (1979, p. 23).

15. School closings are a good example of this problem.

**References**

Alperovich, G. 1979. "The Cost of Living, Labor Market Opportunities and the Migration Decision: A Case of Misspecification?: Comment." *Annals of Regional Science* 13:102–105.

Bowles, S. 1970. "Migration as Investment: Empirical Tests of the Human Investment Approach to Geographic Mobility." *Review of Economics and Statistics* 52:356–362.

Buchanan, J.M. 1950. "Federalism and Fiscal Equity." *American Economic Review* 40:583–599.

Cebula, R.J. 1979. *The Determinants of Human Migration*. Lexington, Mass.: D.C. Heath, Lexington Books.

———. 1981. "The Cost of Living, Labor Market Opportunities, and the Migration Decision: A Case of Misspecification?—A Comment." *Annals of Regional Science*. 15:73–74.

Cebula, R.J., and Vedder, R.K. 1973. "A Note on Migration, Economic Opportunity, and the Quality of Life." *Journal of Regional Science*. 13:205–211.

Cebula, R.J., Kohn, R.M., and Vedder, R.K. 1973. "Some Determinants of Black Interstate Migration, 1965–1970." *Western Economic Journal* 11:500–505.

Gallaway, L.E., and Cebula, R.J. 1972. "Wage-Rate Analysis: Differentials and Indeterminacy." *Industrial and Labor Relations Review* 25: 207–212.

Graves, P.E. 1976. "A Reexamination of Migration, Economic Opportunity, and the Quality of Life." *Journal of Regional Science* 16:107–112.

Greenwood, M.J. 1969. "An Analysis of the Determinants of Geographic Mobility in the United States." *Review of Economics and Statistics* 51: 189–194.

Jones, R.C., and Zannaras, G. 1976. "Perceived versus Objective Urban Opportunities and the Migration of Venezuelan Youths." *Annals of Regional Science* 10:83–97.

Kau, J.B., and Sirmans, C.F. 1976. "New, Repeat, and Return Migration: A Study of Migrant Types." *Southern Economic Journal* 43:1144–1148.

Liu, B.C. 1975. "Differential Net Migration Rates and the Quality of Life." *Review of Economics and Statistics* 57:329–337.

Miller, E. 1973. "Is Out-Migration Affected by Economic Conditions?" *Southern Economic Journal* 39:396–405.

Rabianski, J.S. 1971. "Real Earnings and Human Migration." *Journal of Human Resources* 6:185–192.

Renas, S.M., and Cebula, R.J. 1972. "Investment in Human Capital and the Appropriate Discount Rate." *Social and Economic Studies* 25:61–71.

Renas, S.M., and Kumar, R. 1978. "The Cost of Living, Labor Market Opportunities, and the Migration Decision: A Case of Misspecification?" *Annals of Regional Science* 12:95–104.

———. 1979. "The Cost of Living, Labor Market Opportunities, and the Migration Decision: A Case of Misspecification?: Reply." *Annals of Regional Science* 13:106–108.

———. 1981. "The Cost of Living, Labor Market Opportunities, and the Migration Decision: Some Additional Evidence." *Annals of Regional Science* 15:74–79.

Riew, J. 1973. "Migration and Public Policy." *Journal of Regional Science* 13:65–76.

Schultz, T.W. 1961. "Investment in Human Capital." *American Economic Review* 51:1–17.

Sjaastad, L.A. 1962. "The Costs and Returns of Human Migration." *Journal of Political Economy* 70:Supplement, 80–93.

Vedder, R.K., and Cooper, D. 1974. "Nineteenth-Century English and Welsh Geographic Labor Mobility: Some Further Evidence." *Annals of Regional Science* 8:131–139.

West, D.A., Hamilton, J.R., and Loomis, R.A. 1976. "A Conceptual Framework for Guiding Policy-Related Research on Migration." *Land Economics* 52:66–76.

# Part II
# Determinants of Geographic Living-Cost Differentials

# 2 Determinants of Geographic Living Cost-Differentials: The Basic Model

The first chapter of this book established that there are large and persistent geographic living-cost differentials in the United States; that these differentials have a very significant impact on geographic mobility and regional labor markets in the United States; and that there are (and have been) a number of significant economic and public-policy ramifications of these differentials.

A basic theoretical model is developed in this chapter to help provide insight into the determinants of geographic living-cost differentials. This model will be empirically tested in the following chapter and expanded and modified in subsequent chapters. In the basic model, four hypotheses of potential determinants of living-cost levels are developed: population size, population density, per-capita income, and right-to-work legislation. Once these various hypotheses have been presented, the model will be synthesized.

## Population Size, Agglomeration Economies, and Competition

In any given Standard Metropolitan Statistical Area (SMSA), it may be hypothesized that there are *agglomeration economies* associated with a larger population size. As Isard (1956, p. 182) explains, areas that are subject to agglomeration economies have "access to a larger pool of skilled labor, with fuller use of specialized and auxiliary industrial and repair facilities." He also recognizes that there are economies (efficiencies) that can result from a greater degree of utilization of the "general apparata of an urban structure (such as transportation facilities, gas and water mains . . .) and from a finer articulation of economic activities" (1956, p. 182). Whatever the cause of the agglomeration economy, the end result is a reduction in the costs of production of goods and services.

Among the basic forms agglomeration economies can take are external economies of scale to businesses that are internal to a single industry, and external economies of scale to businesses in many industries. As Nourse (1968) observes, the latter economies have sometimes been known as "urbanization economies." According to Nourse (1968, p. 89), urbanization economies "include the availability of improved transportation services, such as terminal facilities, . . . commercial and financial services, such as banks, . . . and public services, such as fire and police protection.''

Regardless of the form they assume, agglomeration economies ultimately are reflected as downward shifts in the cost curves (the average-cost curves and the marginal-cost curves) of the firms in the industry (industries) affected.[1] This is illustrated in figure 2–1, which shows output per time period plotted along the abscissa and costs (in dollars) plotted along the ordinate axis. The curve $ATC$ is the firm's original average total-cost curve. The curve $ACM$ is the average total-cost curve for the manufacture of specialized machinery that is a part of the firm's final product; clearly, there are significant internal economies of scale in the production of this specialized-machinery component of the firm's final output. As the industry

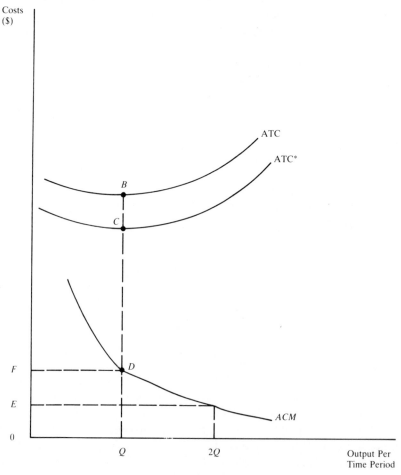

**Figure 2–1.** Agglomeration Economies

of which the firm in question is a part expands, it will very likely become possible for this function (corresponding to $ACM$) to be carried out by separate plants or even separate firms. This possibility arises because of the demand for specialized machinery from many plants or firms. With a larger demand for specialized machinery, the plant producing the specialized machinery can obtain economies of scale in production that any single plant in the original industry could not have attained. Thus, in terms of figure 2–1, the average total cost of producing $Q$ units of output for the original firm may be given by $QB$, and the average total cost of producing $Q$ units of the specialized machinery may be given by $QD$. As the industry grows in size, a specialized plant could produce, say, two $Q$ units of output at an average total cost of, say, $OE$. Since $OE < QD$, the original firm's average total-cost curve shifts downward from $ATC$ to $ATC^*$.[2]

This analysis argues that as an industry expands, average total costs decline; that is, the average total-cost curve shifts downward. Presumably, with population growth in an area and hence a growth in the demand for the output of many industries in the area, a downward shifting of the average total-cost curves of the firms in all of the affected industries should occur.

It now remains to examine the likely effect of agglomeration economies on final-output prices. We will consider two basic types of industrial structure: perfect competition and monopoly.

We analyze the case of competition with the aid of figure 2–2, in which output per time period is measured horizontally and revenues and costs are measured vertically. Originally, the representative firm faces long-run average total-cost curve $ATC_1$, long-run marginal-cost curve $MC_1$, and unit-output price $P_1$. Economic profits in the long run are zero. The occurrence of agglomeration economies leads to a downward shift of curve $ATC_1$ to long-run average-cost curve $ATC_2$ and of curve $MC_1$ to long-run marginal-cost curve $MC_2$. Economic profits become positive. In the long run, positive economic profits elicit entry into the industry, which in turn depresses the market price. In the absence of further agglomeration economies, long-run profits return to zero at price $P_2$. The manifestation of additional agglomeration economies would likely result in a yet lower-cost/lower-price long-run equilibrium. In any event, the existence of agglomeration economies should be expected to result in lower commodity prices in competitive market structures.

Figure 2–3 illustrates the case of monopoly. Output per time period is plotted along the abscissa and revenues and costs are measured along the ordinate axis. The profit-maximizing monopolist is initially shown in long-run equilibrium at the price $P_1$, which was generated by the interaction of its long-run marginal-cost curve $MC_1$ and its marginal-revenue curve $MR$. The appearance of agglomeration economies, as illustrated in figures 2–1 and 2–2, acts to shift the average total-cost curve $ATC_1$ downward, say, in this

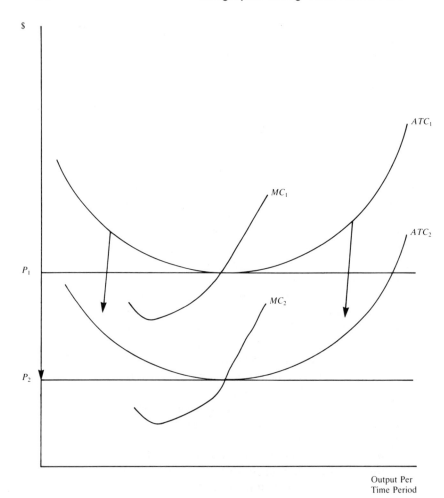

**Figure 2–2.** The Competitive Case

case, to $ATC_2$. The new marginal-cost curve $MC_2$ interacts with the marginal-revenue curve to generate a price of $P_2$. Thus, as was true in the competitive case, agglomeration economies act to reduce final-output prices.[3]

It may be relevant to note that as an area's total population increases, the environment in which its firms and industries operate may become more competitive. In other words, a larger population in an area may incidentally result in increased commodity-market competition in existing industries. In a mildly monopolistic industry, that is, one with a moderate number of firms and some degree of product differentiation but reasonably free entry, increased competition could easily lead to reduced profits and reduced

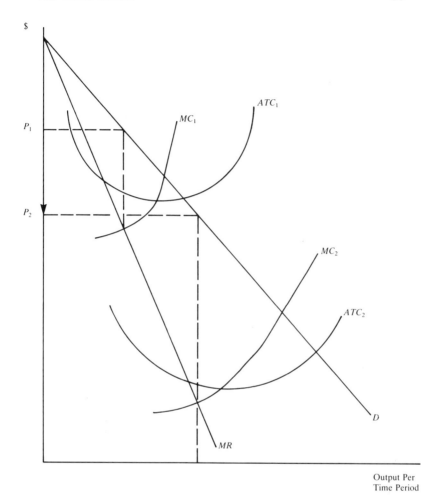

**Figure 2–3.** The Monopolistic Case

prices.[4] The effects of entry on the typical firm in such a case are in part illustrated in figure 2–4. The firm's demand curve has shifted downward from $D_1$ to $D_2$; here, the firm's market share is reduced by intensified competition.

## The Impact of Population Density

We have seen that population size inversely affects the overall cost of living in an area; that agglomeration economies that result from a greater population size act to reduce final-output prices. Population *density* also directly

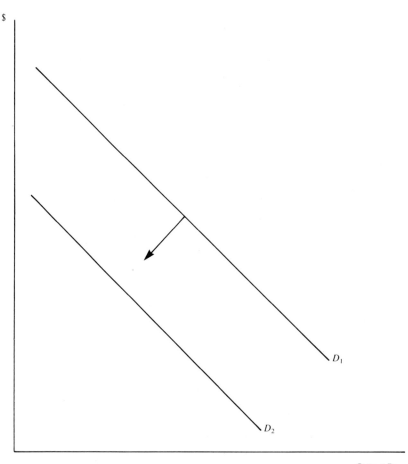

$

$D_1$

$D_2$

Output Per
Time Period

**Figure 2–4.** Effects of Increased Competition

affects the overall cost of living in an area. This direct impact is hypothesized to be the result of two sets of forces: *demand forces* and *transfer diseconomies*.

To see how population density affects the cost of living via its influence on demand, refer to figure 2–5. In figure 2–5, the number of units of housing demanded is plotted horizontally, and the unit price of housing is plotted vertically. The curves $D$ and $D_1$ are both demand curves for housing. Housing quality can be of several different levels; let us assume that there are $n$ different levels of housing quality.[5] The demand curves depicted in

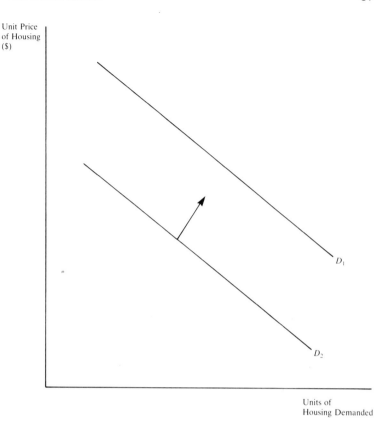

**Figure 2–5.** Demand Curves for Housing of Given Quality

figure 2–5 thus represent two levels of demand for a given level of housing quality.

The demand function implicit in curves $D$ and $D_1$ is given by

$$Dji = Dji \ (Pji, \ Deni, \ . \ . \ .) \qquad (2.1)$$

where

*Dji* is the number of units demanded in area $i$ of housing of quality level $j$; $j = 1, \ . \ . \ . \ , \ n$;

*Pji* is the unit price in area $i$ of housing units of quality level $j$; $j = 1, \ . \ . \ . \ , \ n$; and

*Deni* is the population density in area $i$, that is, the number of persons per square mile in area $i$.

In accord with conventional theory,[6] it is assumed (as illustrated by the negative slopes of curves $D$ and $D_1$ in figure 2–5) that

$$\partial Dji/\partial Pji < 0. \tag{2.2}$$

It will be argued that

$$\partial Dji/\partial Deni > 0 \tag{2.3}$$

or

$$\partial Dji/\partial Deni = 0 \tag{2.4}$$

As the population density in any given area increases, the aggregate number of persons per square mile requiring housing increases. This implies that the demand for housing of a given quality, say $n$, will typically either remain unchanged or increase. It will remain unchanged only if the additional persons in the area in question either move in with persons already residing in the area or if the additional persons gravitate to a housing quality other than level $n$. Eventually, of course, the demand for housing of *some* quality level will have to increase in response to a rising population density. This is illustrated in principle in figure 2–5 by the demand-curve shift from $D$ to $D_1$.

The aggregate demand for housing in area $i$ ($ADi$), is given by

$$ADi = \sum_{j=1}^{n} Dji. \tag{2.5}$$

If any of the $Dji$ changes are positive, there is a positive change in $ADi$.

The aggregate supply of housing in area $i$ is given by

$$ASi = \sum_{j=1}^{n} Sji \tag{2.6}$$

where $ASi$ is the aggregate number of housing units supplied in area $i$, and $Sji$ is the number of housing units of quality level $j$; $j = 1, \ldots , n$, supplied in area $i$.

It may be argued that

$$Sji = Sji \, (Pji, \ldots) \tag{2.7}$$

where $Sji$ and $Pji$ are the same as in equation 2.6.

The restriction on the partial derivative for equation 2.7 is

$$\partial Sji/\partial Pji > 0 \qquad (2.8)$$

or

$$\partial Sji/\partial Pji = 0. \qquad (2.9)$$

In either case, a rise in an area's population density that raises its aggregate housing demand will result in a higher overall market price (per unit) of housing in the area.[7] Thus, through its effects on housing demand (and on the demand for land), a higher population density in an area is argued to raise the overall cost of living in that area.

The population density in an area is also hypothesized here to raise the overall cost of living in the area through transfer diseconomies. Clearly, the greater the population density in an area, the greater the amount of congestion in that area. With a greater degree of congestion, it is argued that transfer diseconomies are encountered and that these transfer diseconomies intensify with further increases in population density. Transfer diseconomies are defined here as the additional costs of transit for employees, transportation of output, and marketing and communication that result from increased congestion.[8] All of these additional congestion-related costs are reflected in upward shifting of affected firms' marginal and average total-cost curves.

In figure 2–6, the effects of transfer diseconomies resulting from increased congestion are examined for competitive markets. Initially, the representative firm is in long-run equilibrium, and the unit price $P_1$ is equal to the long-run average total cost and economic profits are equal to zero. As congestion increases because of rising population density, the long-run average total-cost curve and the long-run marginal-cost curve both shift upward, from $ATC_1$ and $MC_1$ to $ATC_2$ and $MC_2$, respectively. This creates a situation of negative economic profits for the representative firm. This in turn induces exit from the industry and hence a leftward shifting of the industry's supply curve. This raises the unit price of the industry's final output. This process continues until a new long-run equilibrium is established at unit price $P_2$, which equals long-run average total costs. Once again, economic profits become zero. The final effect of the increase in population density has been to raise the final output price (per unit).

The analysis of the effects (on unit-output price) of transfer diseconomies in monopolistic markets is aided by figure 2–7. Initially, the profit-maximizing monopolist is in long-run equilibrium at unit price $P_1$, as determined by the intersection of its marginal-revenue schedule ($MR$) and initial long-run marginal-cost schedule ($MC_1$). As congestion increases from a rise

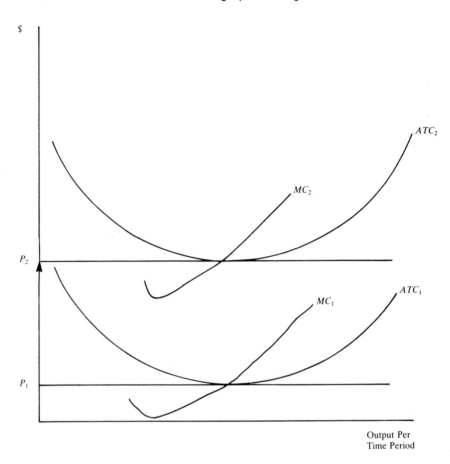

**Figure 2–6.** Transfer Diseconomies in Competitive Markets

in population density, the long-run average total-cost schedule and the long-run marginal-cost schedule shift upward from $ATC_1$ and $MC_1$ to $ATC_2$ and $MC_2$, respectively. The intersection of curve $MC_2$ with the marginal-revenue schedule $MR$ now yields a profit-maximizing unit price of $P_2$. $P_2$ is greater than $P_1$; therefore, we once again conclude (as in the analysis of figure 2–6) that an increase in population density tends to result in a higher output price per unit.

Our findings so far can be summarized as:

1.  Increased population density in an area raises the cost of living in that area by raising the demand for housing (and land).

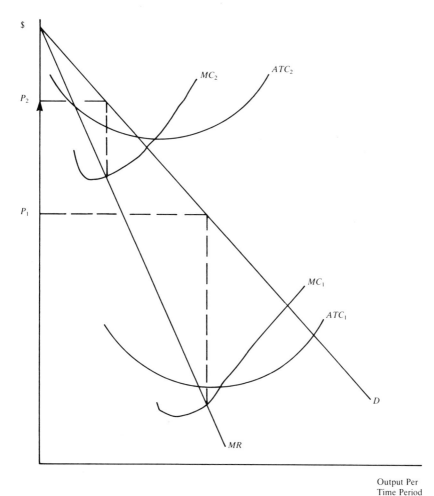

**Figure 2–7.** Transfer Diseconomies in Monopolistic Markets

2.  Increased population density in an area raises the cost of living in that
    area by imposing transfer diseconomies that raise production costs and
    therefore output prices.[9]

    Population density can be defined as

    $$Deni = Popi/Ai \qquad\qquad (2.10)$$

where

*Deni* is the population density, in number of persons per square mile, of area *i*;

*Popi* is the total population in area *i*; and

*Ai* is the number of square miles in area *i*.

A rise in population must result in a rise in population density unless

$$\Delta \ (Popi/Ai) = 0. \qquad (2.11)$$

That is, a rise in population size results in a rise in population density unless the percentage change in the value of *Popi* precisely equals the percentage change in the value of *Ai*. Obviously, the probability of such a condition is rather remote. We should expect population changes to ordinarily result in population-density changes. Since population growth acts to lower the cost of living, whereas population-density growth acts to elevate the cost of living, according to our hypotheses, these opposing forces of population change the population-density change will not, in theory, *entirely* offset one another.[10]

**Income Levels, Demand, and Living Costs**

What are the possible impacts of income on demand for goods and services on the cost of living? The basic argument is simple: higher income levels lead to increased purchasing power; increased purchasing power implies a higher overall level of demand for goods and services; and a higher overall demand for goods and services generally raises commodity prices.

We begin with the consumer who seeks to maximize his utility:

$$U = U \ (Q_1, \ Q_2) \qquad (2.12)$$

subject to his budget constraint

$$DI = (P_1 \cdot Q_1) + (P_2 \cdot Q_2) \qquad (2.13)$$

where

*U* is the utility level for the consumer;

$Q_1$ is the quantity consumed of commodity $Q_1$;

$Q_2$ is the quantity consumed of commodity $Q_2$;

$DI$ is disposable money income;

$P_1$ is the unit price of commodity $Q_1$; and

$P_2$ is the unit price of commodity $Q_2$.

The consumer is shown in an initial equilibrium in figure 2–8 at point $E$.

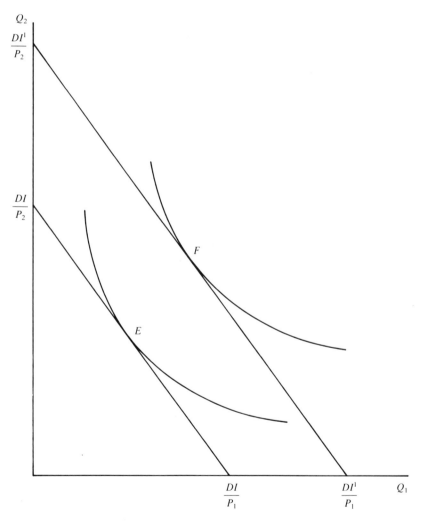

**Figure 2–8.** Consumer Response to Income Change with Normal Goods

If his disposable-money income should rise, his budget line would shift outward from the origin of the diagram and result in a new consumer equilibrium, say at point $F$. The income effect as Lloyd (1967, p. 70) defines it, "the rate of change of consumption of a commodity with respect to income," is assured to be positive in figure 2–8 with respect to both $Q_1$ and $Q_2$:

$$\partial Q_1/\partial DI > 0, \ \partial Q_2/\partial DI > 0. \qquad (2.14)$$

Thus, $Q_1$ and $Q_2$ are normal goods. However, there is no guarantee that, for any given commodity, the income effect will be positive. In other words, the quantity demanded of any commodity, $Q_j$, may not rise with an increase in income. In point of fact, there are three possibilites:

$$\partial Q_j/\partial DI > 0 \qquad (2.15)$$

or

$$\partial Q_j/\partial DI = 0 \qquad (2.16)$$

or

$$\partial Q_j/\partial DI < 0. \qquad (2.17)$$

The quantity demanded of commodity $j$ by individual $i$, $Qji$, may not rise with disposable income. Hence, the quantity demanded of commodity $j$ by the market as a whole (which consists of $m$ individuals) also may not rise with disposable income ($DIi$).

The following possibilities exist with respect to any *single* commodity, $j$:

$$\sum_{i=1}^{m} (\partial Qji/\partial DIi) > 0 \qquad (2.18)$$

or

$$\sum_{i=1}^{m} (\partial Qji/\partial DIi) = 0 \qquad (2.19)$$

or

$$\sum_{i=1}^{m} (\partial Qji/\partial DIi) < 0. \qquad (2.20)$$

Equations 2.18 through 2.20 apply for any *single* commodity in the marketplace.[11] For goods and services as a whole, however, the following must obtain:[12]

$$\sum_{j=1}^{r} \sum_{i=1}^{m} (\partial Qji/\partial DIi) > 0 \qquad (2.21)$$

where the number of commodities is given as $r$, $r \geq 2$.

Thus, as disposable income increases, other things being equal, so does the overall demand for goods and services. So long as Walrasian stability obtains, the end result will be a rise in the overall price of goods and services, that is, a rise in the overall cost of living. Accordingly, the hypothesis developed here states that the *overall* cost of living is an increasing function of the level of per-capita income.[13]

### The Impact of Right-to-Work Laws on Living Costs

Living costs in a region, as we have seen, are affected by population size, population density, and per-capita income levels. They are also determined in part by the presence of right-to-work legislation in the region.

Section 14(b) of the Taft-Hartley Act states that the "union shop" is a legal form of union unless specifically prohibited by state legislation. Each state has the option to adopt or reject such legislation. In point of fact, several states have very recently considered the passage of right-to-work laws; however, there have been no recent additions to the list of states with such legislation. Thus far a total of some nineteen states have legislated right-to-work laws to make compulsory union membership and hence the union shop illegal. The states where right-to-work legislation is currently in force are Alabama, Arizona, Arkansas, Florida, Georgia, Iowa, Kansas, Mississippi, Nebraska, Nevada, North Carolina, North Dakota, South Carolina, South Dakota, Tennessee, Texas, Utah, Virginia, and Wyoming.

It is argued here that the existence of right-to-work laws prohibiting union shops in a region tends to create a labor-market environment with less union power (both actual and potential) and thus an environment with less labor-market pressure on the supply side to increase labor costs. In turn, it is argued that to the degree that right-to-work legislation leads to lower labor costs and therefore to lower production costs, there is likely to be a tendency for final commodity prices to be lower in those regions having right-to-work laws, everything else being equal.

To formalize this argument, consider the profit-maximizing firm. Such a firm seeks to maximize

$$\Pi(Q) = R(Q) - C(Q) \qquad\qquad (2.22)$$

where

$\Pi$ is economic profit;

$R$ is total revenue;

$C$ is total cost; and

$Q$ is output rate per time period.

A *necessary* condition to the maximization of $\Pi(Q)$ is that $C(Q)$ be a minimum for each and every level of $Q$.

Accordingly, the firm is typically faced with a constrained cost-minimization problem such as to minimize

$$C = \sum_{i=1}^{v} PiZi \qquad\qquad (2.23)$$

subject to

$$Q = \langle Q \rangle_{av} \qquad\qquad (2.24)$$

where

$C$ and $Q$ are as in equation 2.22;

$Pi$ is the unit price of input $i$;

$Zi$ is the number of units of input $i$ employed; and

$\langle Q \rangle_{av}$ is any specific output level per time period.

Figure 2–9 illustrates the constrained minimization impounded in equations 2.23 and 2.24 for the simplified case where $v = 2$. The isoquant for output level $\langle Q \rangle_{av}$ is tangent to the isocost line defined by $P_1$ and $P_2$. As shown, given the state of available technology and given factor prices $P_1$ and $P_2$, the minimum cost of production for output rate $\langle Q \rangle_{av}$ is $C_1$ currency units.

Consider now two regions, region A and region B. In region A, there is right-to-work legislation; in region B, there is not. Let $V_1$ refer to labor and let the price of labor in region A be $P_1$. Figure 2–9 may be used to illustrate cost minimization for the *given* firm producing $\langle Q \rangle_{av}$ units of output. Con-

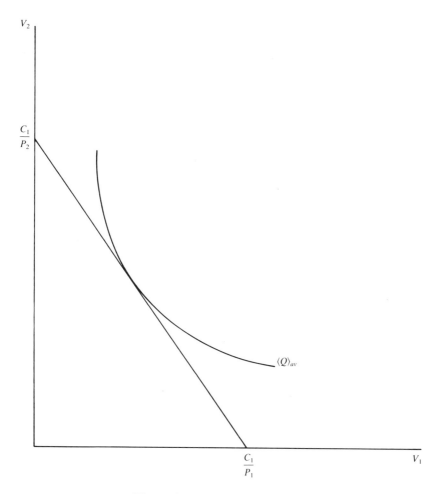

**Figure 2–9.** Cost Minimization

sider the very same problem if the firm is now located in region B. Because of the absence of right-to-work legislation in region B, the price of labor in region B, $P_1^*$, is greater than that in region A. If $P_1^* > P_1$, then so long as $P_2$ is the same in both regions, it follows that

$$C_1/P_1 > C_2/P_1^*. \tag{2.25}$$

From equation 2.25, we infer that the firm's isocost line for region B is closer to the origin along the abscissa of figure 2–9 than it was in region A. Hence, to produce $\langle Q \rangle_{av}$ units of output in region B requires an outlay greater than $C_1$; that is, the total cost of producing $\langle Q \rangle_{av}$ in region B exceeds the total cost of producing $\langle Q \rangle_{av}$ in region A. Since the cost of producing *any* random output $\langle Q \rangle_{av}$ in region B exceeds the cost of producing the same output level in region A, it follows that the firm's total-cost curve in region B lies above that in region A. This is illustrated in figure 2–10, where output per time period is plotted horizontally and total costs in dollars are plotted vertically. Observe that the total-cost curve for region B, $TC_B$, lies everywhere above the total-cost curve for region A, $TC_A$. By extrapolating from figures 2–2 and 2–3, it can be established that the presence of right-to-work laws acts to lower labor costs and thereby results typically in lower output prices.[14] The absence of right-to-work laws, on the other hand, implies higher labor costs and higher output prices.

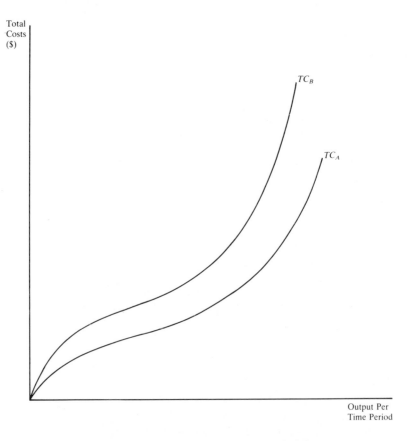

**Figure 2–10.** Total Costs and Right-to-Work Laws

## Summary

This chapter has argued that the cost of living in an area depends, at least in part, on four variables: population size, population density, per-capita income, and right-to-work legislation. The formal model takes the general implicit form:

$$COLi = COLi \ (Popi, \ Deni, \ Inci, \ Righti) \qquad (2.26)$$

where

$COLi$ is overall cost of living in area $i$;

$Popi$ is the total population of area $i$;

$Deni$ is the population density of area $i$;

$Inci$ is the per-capita income in area $i$; and

$Righti$ is an indicator of presence of right-to-work legislation in area $i$.

Based on the various arguments in this chapter, the following signs are imposed on the partial derivatives in equation 2.26:

$$\partial COLi/\partial Popi < 0 \qquad (2.27)$$

$$\partial COLi/\partial Deni > 0 \qquad (2.28)$$

$$\partial COLi/\partial INCi > 0 \qquad (2.29)$$

$$\partial COLi/\partial Righti < 0. \qquad (2.30)$$

In this chapter it has been argued that, other things held the same, the overall cost of living in metropolitan areas is an inverse function of population size. It was hypothesized that agglomeration economies associated with a larger population act to lower production costs. In turn, lower production costs lead to lower output prices. It was also hypothesized that, other things held the same, the overall cost of living in metropolitan areas is a direct function of population density. With increased population density, transfer diseconomies elevate total production and distribution costs. The result of such cost increases is an elevated price structure. Next, it was hypothesized that, other things held the same, the overall cost of living in an area is a direct function of per-capita income. As the per-capita income level rises, so also does the aggregate demand for output. Commodity prices then rise in response to excess demand.

Finally, it was argued that, other things held the same, the overall cost of living in metropolitan areas is an inverse function of the presence of right-to-work legislation. It was hypothesized that right-to-work legislation creates a labor-market environment in which unit labor costs are lower than would be the case in the absence of such legislation. In turn, the lower unit-labor costs associated with right-to-work legislation lead to a lower overall level of output prices.

Chapter 3 will empirically investigate the four sets of hypotheses developed in this chapter.

## Notes

1. Naturally, in the short run, the average and total *fixed*-cost curves would be unaffected by agglomeration economies.

2. Note that $CB = EF = QD - OE$.

3. Naturally, for any given downshifting of an average total-cost curve, the decline in final-output prices would be greater in the competitive market than in the monopolistic market. Hence, the greater the relative degree of competitiveness in an area's commodity markets, the greater the deflationary effects of agglomeration economies.

4. Of course, the consequence of product differentiation would be a negatively sloped demand schedule.

5. Clearly, $n > 1$.

6. We assume housing is not an inferior good; hence, among other things, Gibson's paradox is ruled out. Related to this, see Muth (1961).

7. Assuming a Walrasian stable market, a rising aggregate housing demand will result in a higher unit housing price even if $\partial Sji/\partial Pji < 0$. Related to Walrasian stability, see Bilas (1967, pp. 24–31) and Henderson and Quandt (1958, pp. 110–113).

8. Higher transit costs for employees tend to result in a higher wage structure.

9. This conclusion holds for both the competitive case and the monopolistic case.

10. Obviously, these two sets of forces, by virtue of their being in opposition to one another, must be *partially* offsetting.

11. The issue of the demand for public goods is ignored in the present discussion.

12. This is always true so long as the marginal propensity to consume out of disposable income is positive in the aggregate.

13. Per-capita income is, in reality, a measure of an array of demand-related factors.

14. Labor costs are the complete wage package, that is, wages plus all fringe benefits and other related outlays (such as social-security taxes).

## References

Bilas, R. 1967. *Microeconomic Theory: A Graphical Analysis*. New York: McGraw-Hill.

Henderson, J.M., and Quandt, R.E. 1958. *Microeconomic Theory: A Mathematical Approach*. New York: McGraw-Hill.

Isard, W. 1956. *Location and Space Economy*. Cambridge, Mass.: MIT Press.

Lloyd, C. 1967. *Microeconomic Analysis*. Homewood, Ill.: Irwin.

Muth, R.F. 1961. "The Spatial Structure of the Housing Market." *Papers and Proceedings of the Regional Science Association* 7:207–220.

Nourse, H. 1968. *Regional Economics*. New York: McGraw-Hill.

# 3

# Determinants of Geographic Living Costs: An Empirical Analysis

This chapter is an empirical examination of the hypotheses of chapter 2. The primary analysis involves ordinary least-squares estimations of a linear regression for each of the fourteen years from 1966 through 1979. Sufficient data are available to allow an examination of as many as thirty-nine metropolitan areas. A time-series analysis for Honolulu, Hawaii, is also provided.

In the preceding chapter, it was argued that there are at least four basic determinants of geographic living-cost levels and living-cost differentials in the United States: population size, population density, per-capita income, and right-to-work legislation. These relationships were summarized in equation 2.26 $[COL_i = COL_i (Pop_i, Den_i, Inc_i, Right_i)]$. For mathematical simplicity, we rewrite the equation as

$$C_i = C_i (P_i, D_i, I_i, R_i) \tag{3.1}$$

where

$C_i$ is $COL_i$ (overall living cost in area $i$);

$P_i$ is $Pop_i$ (total population of area $i$);

$D_i$ is $Den_i$ (population density in area $i$);

$I_i$ is $Inc_i$ (per-capita income in area $i$); and

$R_i$ is $Right_i$ (presence of right-to-work legislation in area $i$).

Taking the total differential of equation 3.1 yields

$$dC_i = (\partial C_i/\partial P_i)\, dP_i + (\partial C_i/\partial D_i)\, dD_i + (\partial C_i/\partial I_i)\, dI_i + (\partial C_i/\partial R_i)\, dR_i. \tag{3.2}$$

From the arguments developed in chapter 2, it follows that

$$\partial C_i/\partial P_i < 0 \tag{3.3}$$

$$\partial C_i/\partial D_i > 0 \tag{3.4}$$

$$\partial C_i/\partial I_i > 0 \tag{3.5}$$

$$\partial Ci/\partial Ri < 0. \tag{3.6}$$

To examine equation 3.2 empirically, it must be expressed in linear terms. Accordingly, the general regression-equation form to be estimated in this chapter (by ordinary least squares) is given by

$$Ci = a_0 + a_1Pi + a_2Di + a_3Ii + a_4Ri + \mu \tag{3.7}$$

where

$Ci$, $Pi$, $Di$, $Ii$, and $Ri$ are as in equation 3.1;

$a_0$ is a constant term; and

$\mu$ is a stochastic-error term.

A log-linear version of equation 3.7 would be inappropriate in this analysis since the variable $Ri$ will be represented below by a dummy variable.[1]
From equations 3.3 through 3.7, the following should be expected.

$$\partial Ci/\partial Pi = a_1 < 0 \tag{3.8}$$

$$\partial Ci/\partial Di = a_2 > 0 \tag{3.9}$$

$$\partial Ci/\partial Ii = a_3 > 0 \tag{3.10}$$

$$\partial Ci/\partial Ri = a_4 < 0 \tag{3.11}$$

For simplicity it has been assumed that

$$\partial^2 Ci/\partial Pi^2 = \partial^2 Ci/\partial Di^2 = \partial^2 Ci/\partial Ii^2 = \partial^2 Ci/\partial Ri^2 = 0. \tag{3.12}$$

The conditions summarized in 3.12 follow from the fact that $a_1$, $a_2$, $a_3$, and $a_4$ are all linear terms.[2]

**General Description of Selected Data**

The regression model specified in equation 3.7 is to be estimated for each of the years from 1966 through 1979. Before examining these estimations, however, it would be appropriate for certain of the cost-of-living and population data to be described in some detail.

As noted in the first chapter of this book, there are three basic sets of living-cost data compiled by the U.S. Bureau of Labor Statistics: budgets for low, moderate, and high standards of living. In addition, there are budget figures for retired couples. The present analysis deals exclusively with the budget for a moderate standard of living. It is felt that among the four budget alternatives, the budget for a moderate living standard is likely to be the living-cost measure to which the average member of society best relates.[3]

The living-cost data examined are geographically comparable in view of the general similarity of consumer goods among different areas in the United States. Indeed, this fact is what permits regression analysis to be meaningfully undertaken. Nevertheless, the data have limitations that warrant attention. For one thing, the living-cost data reflect differences in living costs for *established* residents in an area. Rental costs, for instance, are based on the averages for already occupied dwellings. Hence, these rental costs are not an entirely accurate measure of the cost of vacant rental units for *new* residents. In addition, the costs of housing for any given area are in fact an *average;* it is not at all clear that this average is meaningful since the price of housing, even within a given metropolitan area, varies enormously. Moreover, this variance in the price of housing is likely to differ substantially from one metropolitan area to another.

The living-cost data presumably reflect the cost of living for a four-person family, a family consisting of an employed husband (age 38), a wife not employed outside the home, a daughter (age 8), and a son (age 13). To the degree that any given family unit deviates from this norm, the living-cost data lose meaning.

Further, it is not at all obvious that the living-cost data are controlled sufficiently for geographic differences in preference patterns. For instance, there are considerable differences in regional preference patterns in the choice of food to meet nutritional needs.[4] There are even considerable differences within a given metropolitan area in preferences for food. Not only are interregional comparisons of food costs crude, but so too are the average food-cost computations within metropolitan areas. There are also enormous geographic differentials in the preference patterns for clothing (contrast New York City with Los Angeles, California). Thus, in both the categories of food and clothing, the living-cost data are rather crude. On yet another level, there will inevitably be geographic differences in the quality of goods and in the available mix of goods (as some areas can provide snow skiing, while others provide water skiing and warm, sandy beaches). Living-cost data may not be controlled adequately for these differences in location-specific commodities.

A comment regarding the population-size and population-density variables is also appropriate. As noted in equations 3.3 and 3.4, it has been hypothesized that, all else equal, living costs are a decreasing function of population size and an increasing function of population density. In Chapter

2, however, it was shown that a change in population size is very likely to lead to a change in population density as well. Thus, although the a priori arguments in equations 3.3 and 3.4 are founded on an assumption of ceteris paribus (all else being equal), the variables $Pi$ and $Di$ are, in reality, likely to be highly interrelated, and this relationship could well result in multicollinearity problems. This matter of multicollinearity will be addressed in greater detail.

## Empirical Findings, 1966–1979

In this section of the chapter, the empirical results from estimating equation 3.7 by ordinary least squares for each of the years from 1966 through 1979 are presented and analyzed. From 1966 until very recently, there have been thirty-nine Standard Metropolitan Statistical Areas (SMSAs) for which geographically comparable living-cost levels have been compiled by the U.S. Bureau of Labor Statistics. Those SMSAs that are analyzed for most or all of the years from 1966 through 1979 are: Atlanta, Ga.; Austin, Tex.; Bakersfield, Cal.; Baltimore, Md.; Baton Rouge, La.; Boston, Mass.; Buffalo, N.Y.; Champaign–Urbana, Ill.; Cedar Rapids, Iowa; Chicago, Ill.; Cincinnati, Ohio; Cleveland, Ohio; Dallas, Tex.; Dayton, Ohio; Denver, Col.; Detroit, Mich.; Durham, N.C.; Green Bay, Wis.; Hartford, Conn.; Honolulu, Hawaii; Houston, Tex.; Indianapolis, Ind.; Kansas City, Mo.; Lancaster, Pa.; Los Angeles–Long Beach, Cal.; Milwaukee, Wis.; Minneapolis–St. Paul, Minn.; Nashville, Tenn.; New York, N.Y.; Orlando, Fla.; Philadelphia, Pa.; Pittsburgh, Pa.; Portland, Maine; St. Louis, Mo.; San Diego, Cal.; San Francisco–Oakland, Cal.; Seattle–Everett, Wash.; Washington, D.C.; and Wichita, Kans. For most of the years from 1966 through 1979, sufficient data were available to permit an analysis of nearly all of these SMSAs.

### The Year 1966

To investigate formally the determinants of geographic living-cost differentials for the year 1966, we examine the following version of equation 3.7:

$$Ci = b_0 + b_1Pi + b_2Di + b_3Ii + b_4Ri + \mu_1 \qquad (3.13)$$

where

$Ci$ is the average annual cost of living in SMSA $i$ for a four-person family living on an intermediate budget in 1966;

$b_0$ is a constant term;

$Pi$ is the total population in SMSA $i$, 1966;

$Di$ is the population density in SMSA $i$ in 1966, expressed in terms of the number of persons per square mile;

$Ii$ is the per-capita income level in SMSA $i$, 1966;

$Ri$ is a dummy variable that indicates the existence in 1966 of right-to-work legislation in the state where SMSA $i$ is principally located; and

$\mu_1$ is a stochastic-error term.

The variable $Ri$ assumes a value of one if there is right-to-work legislation in the state where SMSA $i$ is principally located; the variable $Ri$ assumes a value of zero if there is not right-to-work legislation in the state where SMSA $i$ is principally located. If SMSA $i$ is located in $j$ states, where $j > 1$, then the $j$th state having the largest percentage of the SMSA's total population is the state used for determining whether or not the SMSA is treated as having right-to-work legislation.[5]

From equations 3.8 through 3.11, it follows that we should expect the following to obtain:

$$b_1 < 0, \; b_2 > 0, \; b_3 > 0, \text{ and } b_4 < 0. \tag{3.14}$$

The ordinary least-squares estimate of regression equation 3.13 is given by

$$Ci = +7032.75 - 0.00017Pi + 0.42165Di + 0.69396Ii - 482.303Ri$$
$$(+10.85) \quad (-2.42) \quad\quad (+2.59) \quad\quad (+3.41) \quad\quad (-2.78)$$

$$R^2 = 0.56 \quad \langle R \rangle_{av}^2 = 0.51 \quad n = 39 \quad DF = 34$$

$$F = 10.7212 \quad \langle C \rangle_{av} i = 9221.95 \tag{3.15}$$

where terms in parentheses beneath coefficients are signed $t$-values.

All four of the estimated coefficients have the expected signs. In addition, the $t$-values of all four of the estimated coefficients are statistically significant at beyond the 0.01 level. The $R^2$ is 0.56, and the $\langle R \rangle_{av}^2$ is 0.51, meaning that the model explains over half of the variation in the cost of living. There were thirty-nine SMSAs for which adequate data were available for analysis; this accounts for the thirty-four degrees of freedom $(DF)$. In addition, the $F$-statistic is statistically significant at the 0.01 level.

The zero-order correlation coefficients among the independent variables are provided in table 3–1. There appear to be three cases of potential multicollinearity problems:

1.  $Pi$ and $Di,$ at +0.89;
2.  $Pi$ and $Ii,$ at +0.57; and
3.  $Di$ and $Ii,$ at +0.51.

However, since the $t$-values of the coefficients for each of the variables involved, $Pi$, $Di$, and $Ii$, are all highly significant, these correlation coefficients should not be a matter of concern.[6]

The results shown in equation 3.15 offer strong empirical support for the hypotheses developed in chapter 2. The coefficient of variable $Pi$ is negative and statistically significant at the 0.01 level. This is entirely consistent with the two-part hypothesis developed in chapter 2 regarding the impact of population size on the overall level of the cost of living. The coefficient on variable $Di$ is positive and statistically significant at the 0.01 level. This result agrees with the two-part hypothesis developed earlier regarding the impact of population density on the cost of living. The coefficient of variable $Ii$ is positive, as hypothesized earlier, and is statistically significant at beyond the 0.01 level. Finally, the coefficient of variable $Ri$ is negative and statistically significant at beyond the 0.01 level. This too conforms to the theoretical analysis in chapter 2.

From the results presented in equation 3.15, it can be inferred, for the year 1966, that the cost of living in an SMSA was an increasing function of both population density and per-capita income. In addition, for the year 1966 the cost of living in an SMSA was a decreasing function of both population size and the existence of right-to-work legislation.

Of the thirty-nine SMSAs examined in equation 3.15, only one—Honolulu, Hawaii,—is not located in the contiguous United States. To determine whether this inclusion may have materially altered the results reported in equation 3.15, we re-estimated equation 3.13 for the year 1966, with Honolulu excluded from the regression. The ordinary least-squares results are given by equation 3.16.

**Table 3–1**
**Correlation Coefficients, 1966**

|      | $Pi$  | $Di$  | $Ii$  | $Ri$ |
|------|-------|-------|-------|------|
| $Pi$ | 1.00  |       |       |      |
| $Di$ | 0.89  | 1.00  |       |      |
| $Ii$ | 0.57  | 0.51  | 1.00  |      |
| $Ri$ | −0.29 | −0.26 | −0.41 | 1.00 |

$$Ci = +6964.95 - 0.00009Pi + 0.24655Di + 0.69349Ii - 397.011Ri$$
$$(+14.94) \quad (-1.70) \quad (+2.04) \quad (+4.74) \quad (-3.16)$$

$$R^2 = 0.68 \quad \langle R \rangle_{av}^2 = 0.64 \quad n = 38 \quad DF = 33$$

$$F = 17.7720 \quad \langle C \rangle_{av} = 9170.16 \tag{3.16}$$

where terms in parentheses are $t$-values.

All of the coefficients have the hypothesized signs. Two coefficients are significant at beyond the 0.01 level; one coefficient is significant at roughly the 0.04 level; and one coefficient is significant at about the 0.07 level. The $R^2$ is 0.68, and the $\langle R \rangle_{av}^2$ is 0.64. The $F$-statistic is significant at far beyond the 0.01 level.[7]

Informally contrasting the results of equations 3.15 and 3.16 reveals no dramatic changes. However, the $F$-statistic, the $R^2$, and the $\langle R \rangle_{av}^2$ are all higher in equation 3.16 than in equation 3.15. In addition, the $t$-values of variables $Ii$ and $Ri$ are higher in equation 3.16 than in equation 3.15. However, the $t$-values of variables $Pi$ and $Di$ are both higher in equation 3.15 than in equation 3.16. All of these differences notwithstanding, the basic results in both regressions are much the same; in particular, the findings in equations 3.15 and 3.16 imply that

$$\partial Ci/\partial Pi < 0 \text{ for 1966, } i = 1, \ldots, 39 \tag{3.17}$$

$$\partial Ci/\partial Di > 0 \text{ for 1966, } i = 1, \ldots, 39 \tag{3.18}$$

$$\partial Ci/\partial Ii > 0 \text{ for 1966, } i = 1, \ldots, 39 \tag{3.19}$$

$$\partial Ci/\partial Ri < 0 \text{ for 1966 } i = 1, \ldots, 39 \tag{3.20}$$

At least for the year 1966, it appears that the inclusion of Honolulu, Hawaii, in the regression analysis (and all of its potentially unique characteristics) has little impact on the basic empirical findings.

*The Year 1967*

To investigate empirically the determinants of geographic living-cost differentials for the year 1967, the following regression is to be estimated:

$$Ci = c_0 + c_1 Pi + c_2 Di + c_3 Ii + c_4 Ri + \mu_2 \tag{3.21}$$

where

Ci is the average annual cost of living in SMSA i for a four-person family living on an intermediate budget in 1967;

$c_0$ is a constant term;

Pi is the total population in SMSA i in 1967;

Di is the population density in SMSA i in 1966, expressed in terms of the number of persons per square mile;

Ii is the 1966 per-capita income level in SMSA i;

Ri is a dummy variable indicating the existence of right-to-work laws in 1967 in the state where SMSA i is principally located; and

$\mu_2$ is a stochastic-error term.

As noted earlier, the value of the dummy variable is given by

$$Ri = 0 \quad \text{or} \quad Ri = 1. \tag{3.22}$$

From equations 3.8 through 3.11, it follows that the following signs on the coefficients in equation 3.21 should be expected:

$$c_1 < 0, \; c_2 > 0, \; c_3 > 0, \text{ and } c_4 < 0. \tag{3.23}$$

The ordinary least-squares estimate of equation 3.21 is given by

$$Ci = +6929.24 - 0.00016Pi + 0.43074Di + 0.67374Ii - 519.89Ri$$
$$\quad\;\; (+9.86) \qquad (-2.30) \qquad\; (+2.51) \qquad\; (+3.12) \qquad\;\; (-2.94)$$

$$R^2 = 0.56 \qquad \langle R \rangle_{av}{}^2 = 0.51 \qquad n = 38 \qquad DF = 33$$

$$F = 10.4878 \qquad \langle C \rangle_{av} i = 9097.66. \tag{3.24}$$

where terms in parentheses beneath coefficients are signed t-values.

All four of the estimated coefficients have the hypothesized signs, and the t-values of all four coefficients are statistically significant at the 0.01 level or beyond. The $R^2$ is 0.56, and the $\langle R \rangle_{av}{}^2$ is 0.51; hence, the model explains more than half of the total variation in the dependent variable. In addition, the F-statistic is significant at well beyond the 0.01 level.

The zero-order correlation coefficients for the exogenous variables in equation 3.24 are provided in table 3–2. Table 3–2 reveals three possible sources of multicollinearity:

**Table 3–2**
**Correlation Coefficients, 1967**

|      | Pi    | Di    | Ii    | Ri   |
|------|-------|-------|-------|------|
| Pi   | 1.00  |       |       |      |
| Di   | 0.90  | 1.00  |       |      |
| Ii   | 0.54  | 0.50  | 1.00  |      |
| Ri   | -0.27 | -0.29 | -0.37 | 1.00 |

1. *Pi* and *Ii,* at +0.54;
2. *Di* and *Ii,* at +0.50; and
3. *Pi* and *Di,* at +0.90.

These high correlation coefficients notwithstanding, the strength of the *t*-values on the coefficients for *Pi, Ii,* and *Di* leaves little about which to be concerned.

The empirical findings indicated in equation 3.24 lend strong support to the four hypotheses developed in chapter 2 regarding the determinants of geographic living-cost differentials. The coefficient of *Pi* is negative, as hypothesized, and statistically significant at roughly the 0.01 level. The coefficient of variable *Di* is positive, as expected, and statistically significant at beyond the 0.01 level. The coefficient of variable *Ii* is positive, as hypothesized, and statistically significant at far beyond the 0.01 level. Finally, as expected, the coefficient of variable *Ri* is negative and statistically significant at well beyond the 0.01 level.

These findings lead to the following conclusions for the year 1967: the cost of living was an increasing function of population density and per-capita income; and the cost of living was a decreasing function of population size and the presence of right-to-work laws. These results are consistent with those reported for the year 1966 in equation 3.15.

The exclusion of Honolulu from the first regression was found to have little impact on the overall empirical findings for 1966 (see equations 3.15 and 3.16). However, this is not the case for the year 1967. Equation 3.27 provides the ordinary least-squares estimate of equation 3.21, with Honolulu excluded from the analysis:

$$Ci = +6758.34 - 0.00083Pi + 0.24452Di + 0.70735Ii - 454.068Ri$$
$$(+12.78) \quad (-1.51) \quad (+1.83) \quad (+4.35) \quad (-3.40)$$

$$R^2 = 0.67 \quad \langle R \rangle_{av}^2 = 0.63 \quad n = 37 \quad DF = 32$$

$$F = 16.3703 \quad \langle C \rangle_{av}i = 9048.89. \tag{3.25}$$

where terms in parentheses are *t*-values.

Contrasting the results in equation 3.25 with those in equation 3.24 reveals that if Honolulu, Hawaii, is excluded from the regression, the *t*-values of both the variable $Pi$ and the variable $Di$ decline dramatically. In fact, in equation 3.25, $Di$ is barely statistically significant at the 0.06 level, and $Pi$ fails to be statistically significant at even the 0.10 level. Hence, the strength of two of our basic hypotheses has been thrown into question. The estimations for following years should help shed further light on this issue.

*The Year 1968*

For the year 1968, the regression equation to be estimated is given by

$$Ci = d_0 + d_1 Pi + d_2 Di + d_3 Ii + d_4 Ri + \mu_3 \qquad (3.26)$$

where

$Ci$ is the average annual cost of living in SMSA *i* for a four-person family living on an intermediate budget in 1968;

$d_0$ is a constant term;

$Pi$ is the total population in SMSA *i* in 1968

$Di$ is the population density in SMSA *i* in 1968, expressed in terms of the number of persons per square mile;

$Ii$ is the 1968 per-capita income in SMSA *i;*

$Ri$ is a dummy variable indicating the existence of right-to-work laws in 1968 in the state where SMSA *i* is principally located; and

$\mu_3$ is a stochastic-error term.

From equations 3.8 through 3.11, the following signs of the coefficients in equation 3.26 should be anticipated:[8]

$$d_1 < 0, \ d_2 > 0, \ d_3 > 0, \text{ and } d_4 < 0. \qquad (3.27)$$

The ordinary least-squares estimate of regression equation 3.26 is given by

$$Ci = +7157.03 - 0.00017Pi + 0.41603Di + 0.54506Ii - 557.312Ri$$
$$\quad (+9.47) \qquad (-2.48) \qquad (+2.47) \qquad (+2.66) \qquad (-3.29)$$

$$R^2 = 0.58 \qquad \langle R \rangle_{av}^2 = 0.53 \qquad n = 39 \qquad DF = 34$$

$$F = 11.6418 \qquad \langle C \rangle_{av} i = 9085.95 \tag{3.28}$$

where terms in parentheses beneath coefficients are signed $t$-values.

All of the estimated coefficients have the expected signs; moreover, the $t$-values of all four of the estimated coefficients are statistically significant at well beyond the 0.01 level. The $R^2$ is 0.58 and the $\langle R \rangle_{av}^2$ is 0.53, so that the model once again explains more than half of the variation in the dependent variable. Finally, the $F$-ratio is statistically significant at beyond the 0.01 level.

The zero-order correlation coefficients among the independent variables in equation 3.28 are shown in table 3–3. In all, there are four possible sources of multicollinearity problems:

1. $Pi$ and $Ii$, at $+0.66$;
2. $Di$ and $Ii$, at $+0.61$;
3. $Ri$ and $Ii$, at $-0.51$; and
4. $Pi$ and $Di$, at $+0.91$.

Ordinarily, such high values for correlation coefficients are a source of potential trouble; however, the enormous strength of all of the $t$-values in equation 3.28 indicates that there are no *actual* multicollinearity problems in the regression.

Estimating equation 3.26 for the year 1968 excluding Honolulu, Hawaii, yields results that are remarkably similar to those in equation 3.28. We can infer that for the year 1968, the cost of living in SMSAs was an increasing function of population density and per-capita income and a decreasing function of population size and the presence of right-to-work laws, *supporting* the hypotheses developed in chapter 2.

*The Year 1969*

The regression equation to be estimated for the year 1969 is given by

**Table 3–3**
**Correlation Coefficients, 1968**

|  | Pi | Di | Ii | Ri |
|---|---|---|---|---|
| Pi | 1.00 | | | |
| Di | 0.91 | 1.00 | | |
| Ii | 0.66 | 0.61 | 1.00 | |
| Ri | −0.32 | −0.30 | −0.51 | 1.00 |

$$Ci = e_0 + e_1Pi + e_2Di + e_3Ii + e_4Ri + \mu_4 \qquad (3.29)$$

where

$Ci$ is the average annual cost of living in SMSA $i$ for a four-person family living on an intermediate budget in 1969;

$e_0$ is a constant term;

$Pi$ is the total population in SMSA $i$ in 1968;

$Di$ is the population density in SMSA $i$ in 1968, expressed in terms of the number of persons per square mile;

$Ii$ is the per-capita income level in SMSA $i$ in 1969;

$Ri$ is a dummy variable that indicates the presence of right-to-work legislation in 1968 in the state where SMSA $i$ is principally located; and

$\mu_4$ is a stochastic-error term.

The expected signs of the coefficients in equation 3.29 are as follows:

$$e_1 < 0, \; e_2 > 0, \; e_3 > 0, \text{ and } e_4 < 0. \qquad (3.30)$$

The ordinary least-squares estimate of regression equation 3.29 is given by

$$Ci = +7723.87 - 0.00019Pi + 0.55995Di + 0.70180Ii - 645.336Ri$$
$$\phantom{Ci =} (+8.73) \qquad (-2.38) \qquad (+2.87) \qquad (+2.62) \qquad (-3.38)$$

$$R^2 = 0.58 \qquad \langle R \rangle_{av}{}^2 = 0.53 \qquad n = 39 \qquad DF = 34$$

$$F = 11.8032 \qquad \langle C \rangle_{av}i = 10063.51 \qquad\qquad (3.31)$$

where terms in parentheses below coefficients are $t$-values.

All four of the estimated coefficients have the expected signs, and the $t$-values of all of the coefficients are statistically significant at the 0.01 level or beyond. The $R^2$ is 0.58, and the $\langle R \rangle_{av}{}^2$ is 0.53; this means that the model explains well over half of the variation in the level of the cost of living. Finally, the $F$-statistic is statistically significant at well beyond the 0.01 level.

The zero-order correlation coefficients among the independent variables in equation 3.31 are provided in table 3–4. As shown in the table, there are three cases of possible multicollinearity:

**Table 3–4**
**Correlation Coefficients, 1969**

|      | Pi    | Di    | Ii    | Ri   |
|------|-------|-------|-------|------|
| Pi   | 1.00  |       |       |      |
| Di   | 0.91  | 1.00  |       |      |
| Ii   | 0.58  | 0.55  | 1.00  |      |
| Ri   | −0.28 | −0.30 | −0.34 | 1.00 |

1.  $Pi$ and $Di$, at +0.91;
2.  $Pi$ and $Ii$, at +0.58; and
3.  $Ii$ and $Di$, at +0.55.

These high values for correlation coefficients should not be of major concern because the coefficients for all of the variables concerned are statistically significant in equation 3.31 at beyond the 0.01 level.

Estimating equation 3.29 by ordinary least squares, excluding Honolulu from the data base, yields equation 3.32:

$$Ci = +7875.79 - 0.00010Pi + 0.36937Di + 0.63800Ii - 597.072Ri$$
$$(+10.78) \quad (-1.46) \quad (+2.21) \quad (+2.88) \quad (-3.78)$$

$$R^2 = 0.63 \quad \langle R \rangle_{av}^2 = 0.59 \quad n = 38 \quad DF = 33$$

$$F = 14.2782 \quad \langle C \rangle_{av}i = 10009.53 \tag{3.32}$$

where terms in parentheses are $t$-values.

Contrasting regression equations 3.31 and 3.32 indicates little change with respect to the variables $Ii$ and $Ri$ in terms of their levels of statistical significance. The $t$-values of the coefficients for variables $Pi$ and $Di$, however, fall substantially once Honolulu is dropped from the data pool. In fact, the coefficient of variable $Pi$ becomes statistically insignificant at even the 0.10 level in equation 3.32. Other differences between the two estimations include higher $R^2$ and $\langle R \rangle_{av}^2$ values in equation 3.32 and a higher $F$-ratio in equation 3.32 as well.

Although the final findings relative to variable $Pi$ are not entirely clear and conclusive, the results presented in equations 3.31 and 3.32 tentatively imply, for the year 1969, that the cost of living in SMSAs was directly related to population density and per-capita income levels, and the cost of living in SMSAs was inversely related to population size and the presence of right-to-work legislation. These results are basically compatible with those for the years 1966, 1967, and 1968.

## The Year 1970

The regression equation to be estimated for the year 1970 is

$$Ci = f_0 + f_1 Pi + f_2 Di + f_3 Ii + f_4 Ri + \mu_5 \tag{3.33}$$

where

Ci is the average annual cost of living in SMSA i for a four-person family living on an intermediate budget in 1970;

$f_0$ is a constant term;

Pi is the total population in SMSA i in 1970;

Di is the population density in SMSA i in 1970, expressed in terms of the number of persons per square mile;

Ii is the 1970 per-capita income level in SMSA i;

Ri is a dummy variable that indicates the presence of right-to-work laws in 1970 in the state in which SMSA i is principally located; and

$\mu_5$ is a stochastic-error term.

On the basis of the analysis of equations 3.8 through 3.11, it follows that the expected signs on the coefficients in equation 3.33 are

$$f_1 < 0, \ f_2 > 0, \ f_3 > 0, \text{ and } f_4 < 0. \tag{3.34}$$

Estimating regression equation 3.33 by ordinary least squares yields the following results.

$$Ci = +7458.99 - 0.00023Pi + 0.54810Di + 0.77017Ii - 622.949Ri$$
$$\quad\ (+9.05) \qquad (-3.50) \qquad\ (+3.71) \qquad\ (+3.77) \qquad\ (-3.33)$$

$$R^2 = 0.71 \qquad \langle R \rangle_{av}^2 = 0.67 \qquad n = 39 \qquad DF = 34$$

$$F = 20.6149 \qquad \langle C \rangle_{av} i = 10644.31 \tag{3.35}$$

where terms in parentheses beneath coefficients are signed t-values.

In equation 3.35, all four of the estimated coefficients have the expected signs; furthermore, the $t$-values of all four of the coefficients are statistically significant at far beyond the 0.01 level. The $R^2$ is 0.71, and the $\langle R \rangle_{av}^2$ is 0.67; therefore, the model explains over two-thirds of the variation in the value of the dependent variable $Ci$ for the year 1970. This is a far better explanatory power than obtained in any of the earlier estimates.[9] Finally, the $F$-ratio is statistically significant at well beyond the 0.01 level.

The zero-order correlation coefficients among the exogenous variables in regression equation 3.35 are provided in table 3–5. As table 3–5 indicates, there are three possible multicollinearity problems. These three cases are given by

1. *Pi* and *Di*, at +0.87;
2. *Di* and *Ii*, at +0.68; and
3. *Pi* and *Ii*, at +0.68.

Typically, such high correlation coefficients would be worrisome; however, the statistical significance of the variables in equation 3.35 is so high that there need not be any major concern.

The ordinary least-squares estimate of equation 3.33 excluding Honolulu from the data base yields results that are nearly identical to those in equation 3.35.[10] On the basis of the findings in regression estimate 3.35, the following conclusions can be made with respect to the year 1970: the cost of living in SMSAs was directly related to both population density and per-capita income levels, and the cost of living in SMSAs was inversely related to both population size and the presence of right-to-work legislation.

*The Year 1971*

The regression equation to be used to explain the determinants of geographic living-cost differentials for the year 1971 is

**Table 3–5**
**Correlation Coefficients, 1970**

|  | Pi | Di | Ii | Ri |
|---|---|---|---|---|
| Pi | 1.00 | | | |
| Di | 0.87 | 1.00 | | |
| Ii | 0.68 | 0.68 | 1.00 | |
| Ri | −0.31 | −0.28 | −0.42 | 1.00 |

$$Ci = g_0 + g_1 Pi + g_2 Di + g_3 Ii + g_4 Ri + \mu_6 \qquad (3.36)$$

where

$Ci$ is the average annual cost of living in SMSA $i$ for a four-person family living on an intermediate budget in 1971;

$g_0$ is a constant term;

$Pi$ is the total population in SMSA $i$ in 1971;

$Di$ is the population density in SMSA $i$ in 1971, expressed in terms of the number of persons per square mile;

$Ii$ is the 1971 per-capita income level in SMSA $i$;

$Ri$ is a dummy variable indicating the presence of right-to-work laws in 1971 in the state where SMSA $i$ is principally located; and

$\mu_6$ is a stochastic-error term.

The expected signs on the coefficients in equation 3.36 are

$$g_1 < 0, \; g_2 > 0, \; g_3 > 0, \text{ and } g_4 < 0. \qquad (3.37)$$

These signs are obviously predicated upon the hypotheses developed in chapter 2.

The ordinary least-squares estimate of equation 3.36 is given by

$$Ci = +8382.29 - 0.00025 Pi + 0.79321 Di + 0.74349 Ii - 647.156 Ri$$
$$\quad\;\; (+7.54) \qquad (-2.90) \qquad (+3.85) \qquad (+2.21) \qquad (-2.86)$$

$$R^2 = 0.59 \qquad \langle R \rangle_{av}^2 = 0.54 \qquad n = 39 \qquad DF = 34$$

$$F = 12.0655 \qquad \langle C \rangle_{av} i = 10952.24 \qquad\qquad (3.38)$$

where terms in parentheses are $t$-values.

In regression estimate 3.38, all four of the estimated coefficients have the expected signs. In addition, the $t$-values of three of the four coefficients are statistically significant at the 0.01 level or beyond (the $t$-value of the remaining coefficient for variable $Ii$ is statistically significant at roughly the 0.025 level). The $R^2$ value is 0.59, and $\langle R \rangle_{av}^2$ is 0.54, so that the model explains nearly three-fifths of the variation in the cost-of-living variable. The overall strength of the equation is verified by the very highly significant $F$-statistic.[11]

The zero-order correlation coefficients among the exogenous variables in regression equation 3.38 are presented in table 3–6. As so often has been the case in these regressions, there are multiple instances of possible multicollinearity problems. The three such cases that derive from the regression for 1971 are

1. $Pi$ and $Ii$, at $+0.58$;
2. $Di$ and $Ii$, at $+0.55$; and
3. $Pi$ and $Di$, at $+0.87$.

Given the strength of the coefficients in regression estimate 3.38, these correlation levels do not seem to be of critical importance. Nevertheless, the fact that the variable $Ii$ is highly correlated with both $Pi$ and $Di$ is what very likely accounts for its relatively low $t$-value in regression 3.38.

Estimating equation 3.36 by ordinary least squares, excluding Honolulu, yields the following results:

$$Ci = +8574.16 - 0.00017Pi + 0.64653Di + 0.65973Ii - 574.712Ri$$
$$(+9.50) \qquad (-2.40) \qquad (+3.79) \qquad (+2.41) \qquad (-3.12)$$

$$R^2 = 0.65 \qquad \langle R \rangle_{av}^2 = 0.60 \qquad n = 38 \qquad DF = 33$$

$$F = 15.0545 \qquad \langle C \rangle_{av}i = 10882.04 \tag{3.39}$$

where terms in parentheses are $t$-values.

Contrasting results of equations 3.38 and 3.39 reveals a number of differences. In equation 3.39, the income variable ($Ii$) is statistically significant at the 0.01 level, whereas the same variable in equation 3.38 is statistically significant at only the 0.025 level. The values for $R^2$ and $\langle R \rangle_{av}^2$ are both a good bit higher in equation 3.39 than in equation 3.38. In addition, the $F$-ratio is significantly higher in equation 3.39 than in equation 3.38.

The differences between regressions 3.38 and 3.39 notwithstanding, there are a number of strong general inferences that can be drawn from these

**Table 3–6**
**Correlation Coefficients, 1971**

|      | $Pi$   | $Di$   | $Ii$   | $Ri$ |
|------|--------|--------|--------|------|
| $Pi$ | 1.00   |        |        |      |
| $Di$ | 0.87   | 1.00   |        |      |
| $Ii$ | 0.58   | 0.55   | 1.00   |      |
| $Ri$ | −0.30  | −0.33  | −0.33  | 1.00 |

results. In particular, for the year 1971, it can be concluded that the cost of living in SMSAs was an increasing function of population density and per-capita income levels, and the cost of living in SMSAs was a decreasing function of population size and the presence of right-to-work legislation.

*The Year 1972*

For the year 1972, the following regression is to be estimated by ordinary least squares:

$$Ci = h_0 + h_1 Pi + h_2 Di + h_3 Ii + h_4 Ri + \mu_7 \qquad (3.40)$$

where

$Ci$ is the average annual cost of living in SMSA $i$ in 1972, for a four-person family living on an intermediate budget;

$h_0$ is a constant term;

$Pi$ is the total population in SMSA $i$ in 1972;

$Di$ is the population density in SMSA $i$ in 1972, expressed in terms of the number of persons per square mile;

$Ii$ is the 1972 per-capita income level in SMSA $i$;

$Ri$ is a dummy variable used to indicate whether or not there were right-to-work laws in 1972 in the state where SMSA $i$ is principally located; and

$\mu_7$ is a stochastic-error term.

On the basis of the analysis impounded in equations 3.8 through 3.11, the following is to be expected:

$$h_1 < 0, \ h_2 > 0, \ h_3 > 0, \ \text{and} \ h_4 < 0. \qquad (3.41)$$

The ordinary least-squares estimate of regression equation 3.40 is given by

$$Ci = +9164.55 - 0.00020Pi + 0.75601Di + 0.43154Ii - 699.854Ri$$
$$(+8.47) \quad (-2.71) \quad (+4.51) \quad (+1.85) \quad (-3.16)$$

$$R^2 = 0.66 \qquad \langle R \rangle_{av}^2 = 0.62 \qquad n = 39 \qquad DF = 34$$

$$F = 16.2365 \qquad \langle C \rangle_{av} i = 11372.63 \tag{3.42}$$

where terms in parentheses beneath coefficients are $t$-values.

In equation estimate 3.42, all four of the estimated coefficients have the expected signs. In addition, three of the four coefficients are statistically significant at the 0.01 level, whereas one coefficient (that corresponding to the income variable, $Ii$) is statistically significant at only the 0.06 level. The $R^2$ is 0.66, and the $\langle R \rangle_{av}^2$ is 0.62, so that the model explains nearly two-thirds of the variation in the endogenous variable. Finally, the $F$-statistic is significant at far beyond the 0.01 level.

The zero-order correlation coefficients among the independent variables in equation 3.42 are provided in table 3–7. There are three potential multicollinearity problems:

1.  $Pi$ and $Ii$, at +0.66;
2.  $Di$ and $Ii$, at +0.60; and
3.  $Di$ and $Pi$, at +0.82.

The income variable, $Ii$, is involved in two of these cases; this very likely accounts for the poor performance of this variable in the estimated regression.

Estimating equation 3.40 by ordinary least squares and excluding Honolulu from the data base yields the following equation:

$$Ci = +10024.61 - 0.00013Pi + 0.67206Di + 0.22963Ii - 696.035Ri$$
$$\quad\; (+10.21) \qquad (-1.87) \qquad (+4.51) \qquad (+1.08) \qquad (-3.59)$$

$$R^2 = 0.69 \qquad \langle R \rangle_{av}^2 = 0.65 \qquad n = 38 \qquad DF = 33$$

$$F = 18.0235 \qquad \langle C \rangle_{av} i = 11313.60 \tag{3.43}$$

where terms in parentheses are $t$-values.

**Table 3–7**
**Correlation Coefficients, 1972**

|      | $Pi$  | $Di$  | $Ii$  | $Ri$ |
|------|-------|-------|-------|------|
| $Pi$ | 1.00  |       |       |      |
| $Di$ | 0.82  | 1.00  |       |      |
| $Ii$ | 0.66  | 0.60  | 1.00  |      |
| $Ri$ | −0.27 | −0.31 | −0.39 | 1.00 |

In equation 3.43, the income variable becomes statistically insignificant at even the 0.10 level; in equation 3.42, the same variable was statistically significant at the 0.06 level. Although the variables $Di$ and $Ri$ are strong in both equations 3.42 and 3.43, the population-size variable ($Pi$) is much weaker in equation 3.43 than in equation 3.42. Finally, the values of the $R^2$, $\langle R \rangle_{av}^2$, and $F$-ratio are all higher in regression-estimate 3.43 than in regression-estimate 3.42.

The somewhat mixed results in equations 3.42 and 3.43 leads to the tentative conclusions that the cost of living in SMSAs during 1972 was an increasing function of population density, and the cost of living in SMSAs in 1972 was a decreasing function of population size and the presence of right-to-work laws.[12]

### The Year 1973

To investigate the determinants of geographic living-cost differentials during the year 1973, the following regression equation is to be estimated:[13]

$$Ci = j_0 + j_1 Pi + j_2 Di + j_3 Ii + j_4 Ri + \mu_8 \qquad (3.44)$$

where

Ci is the average annual cost of living in SMSA $i$ in 1973, for a four-person family living on an intermediate budget;

$j_0$ is a constant term;

$Pi$ is the total population in SMSA $i$ in 1973;

$Di$ is the population density in SMSA $i$ in 1973, expressed in terms of the number of persons per square mile;[14]

$Ii$ is the per-capita income level in SMSA $i$ in 1973;

$Ri$ is a dummy variable used to indicate the presence of right-to-work laws in 1973 in the state where SMSA $i$ is principally located; and

$\mu_8$ is a stochastic-error term.

Only thirty-six SMSAs are considered in this section because of a lack of needed data for Boston, Mass; Hartford, Conn., and Durham, N.C.

The expected signs of the coefficients in equation 3.44 are as follows:

$$j_1 < 0, \ j_2 > 0, \ j_3 > 0, \text{ and } j_4 < 0. \qquad (3.45)$$

The ordinary least-squares estimate of equation 3.44 is given by

$$Ci = +10205.37 - 0.00021Pi + 0.73498Di + 0.33019Ii - 799.041Ri$$
$$\quad (+9.91) \qquad (-2.31) \qquad (+4.10) \qquad (+1.63) \qquad (-3.20)$$

$$R^2 = 0.57 \qquad \langle R \rangle_{av}^2 = 0.53 \qquad n = 36 \qquad DF = 31$$

$$F = 11.9881 \qquad \langle C \rangle_{av}i = 12806.19 \tag{3.46}$$

where terms in parentheses are $t$-values.

   In equation 3.46, all four coefficients have the expected signs. In addition, two of the four coefficients are statistically significant at beyond the 0.01 level, whereas a third coefficient (for $Pi$) is statistically significant at roughly the 0.02 level. The income variable ($Ii$) is statistically significant at only the 0.10 level. The $R^2$ value is 0.57, and the $\langle R \rangle_{av}^2$ is 0.53; hence the model explains over half of the variation in the endogenous variable. The $F$-ratio is statistically significant at the 0.01 level.
   Since there is only one source of possible multicollinearity in this estimation, the correlation matrix is not provided here. The single case of possible concern involves a zero-order correlation coefficient of +0.82 between variables $Pi$ and $Di$. As mentioned earlier in this chapter and in the preceding chapter, it should be expected that $Pi$ and $Di$ are highly correlated. In view of the magnitudes of the $t$-values of these two variables in estimate 3.46, however, it would appear that the multicollinearity issue should not be of concern here. The findings provided in equation 3.46 are almost entirely unchanged if Honolulu is dropped from the analysis.
   For the year 1973, it can be inferred that the cost of living in SMSAs was directly related to population density, and the cost of living in SMSAs was inversely related to population size and the presence of right-to-work laws. The insignificance of the income variable in 1973 is similar to the findings obtained for 1972.

*The Year 1974*

The empirical investigation of the determinants of geographic living-cost levels for the year 1974 postulates the following regression equation:

$$Ci = k_0 + k_1Pi + k_2Di + k_3Ii + k_4Ri + \mu_9 \tag{3.47}$$

where

$C_i$ is the average annual cost of living in SMSA $i$ in 1974, for a four-person family living on an intermediate budget;

$k_0$ is a constant term;

$P_i$ is the total population in SMSA $i$ in 1974;[15]

$D_i$ is the population density in SMSA $i$ in 1973, expressed in terms of the number of persons per square mile;

$I_i$ is the 1974 per-capita income level in SMSA $i$;

$R_i$ is a dummy variable indicating the presence of right-to-work legislation in 1974 in the state where SMSA $i$ is principally located; and

$\mu_9$ is a stochastic-error term.

Because of lack of needed data, Durham, N.C., was omitted from the regression base for 1974 and only thirty-eight SMSAs were examined.

On the basis of the analysis of equations 3.8 through 3.11, the following signs are expected on the coefficients in equation 3.47:

$$k_1 < 0,\ k_2 > 0,\ k_3 > 0,\ \text{and}\ k_4 < 0. \tag{3.48}$$

The ordinary least-squares estimate of equation 3.47 is given by

$$C_i = +13115.14 - 0.00021P_i + 0.76197D_i + 0.24917I_i - 824.46R_i$$
$$\quad\ (+12.37)\quad\ (-1.99)\quad\quad (+4.08)\quad\quad (+1.07)\quad\quad (-3.96)$$

$$R^2 = 0.60\quad\ \langle R \rangle_{av}^2 = 0.55\quad\ n = 38\quad\ DF = 37$$

$$F = 12.2161\quad\ \langle C \rangle_{av}i = 14239.71 \tag{3.49}$$

where terms in parentheses beneath coefficients are signed $t$-values.

In equation 3.49, all four estimated coefficients have the hypothesized signs. Two of the estimated coefficients, those for variables $D_i$ and $R_i$, are statistically significant at the 0.01 level, whereas the coefficient for variable $P_i$ is statistically significant at beyond the 0.05 level. As was the case for the years 1972 and 1973, the income variable is weak; it is not even significant in equation 3.49 at the 0.10 level. The $R^2$ is 0.60, and the $\langle R \rangle_{av}^2$ is 0.55, so that the model explains nearly three-fifths of the variation in the cost-of-living variable. The $F$-ratio is statistically significant at the 0.01 level.

For the year 1973, only one possible multicollinearity problem existed. The same is true for the present year, 1974. The one case involves a zero-order correlation coefficient of $+0.82$ between the variables $Pi$ and $Di$. Since both of these variables performed very well in equation 3.49, the theoretical multicollinearity issue is unimportant.

Estimating regression equation 3.47 by ordinary least squares, omitting Honolulu from the analysis, yields the following:

$$Ci = +13635.13 - 0.00011Pi + 0.62280Di + 0.10566Ii - 117.59Ri$$
$$(+14.26) \quad (-1.18) \quad (+3.63) \quad (+0.50) \quad (-4.05)$$

$$R^2 = 0.62 \quad \langle R \rangle_{av}^2 = 0.58 \quad n = 37 \quad DF = 32$$

$$F = 13.3254 \quad \langle C \rangle_{av}i = 14164.50 \tag{3.50}$$

where terms in parentheses are $t$-values.

In estimate 3.50, all four coefficients have the expected signs, but only two (those for variables $Di$ and $Ri$) are statistically significant at any acceptable level.[16] The coefficients on both variables $Pi$ and $Ii$ fail to be significant at even the 0.10 level. The $R^2$ is 0.62, and the $\langle R \rangle_{av}^2$ is 0.58, so that the model explains roughly three-fifths of the variation in the dependent variable.[17]

The findings in equations 3.49 and 3.50 are generally less powerful than those obtained for the earlier years. Nevertheless, on the basis of equations 3.49 and 3.50, it can be inferred that the cost of living in SMSAs during 1974 was a decreasing function of the presence of right-to-work laws; and the cost of living in SMSAs in 1974 was an increasing function of population density.

*The Year 1975*

The regression equation to be estimated for the year 1975 is as follows:

$$Ci = l_0 + l_1Pi + l_2Di + l_3Ii + l_4Ri + \mu_{10} \tag{3.51}$$

where

Ci is the average annual cost of living in SMSA $i$ in 1975, for a four-person family living on an intermediate budget;

$l_0$ is a constant term;

$Pi$ is the total population in SMSA $i$ in 1975;

$Di$ is the population density in SMSA $i$ in 1975, expressed as the number of persons per square mile;

$Ii$ is the 1975 per-capita income level in SMSA $i$;

$Ri$ is a dummy variable indicating the presence of right-to-work laws in 1975 in the state where SMSA $i$ is principally located; and

$\mu_{10}$ is a stochastic-error term.

Because of a lack of needed data, the SMSAs of Boston, Mass., Durham, N.C., and Pittsburgh, Pa. are omitted, and only thirty-six SMSAs are analyzed for the year 1975.

The expected signs of the coefficients in equation 3.51 are:

$$l_1 < 0, \; l_2 > 0, \; l_3 > 0, \text{ and } l_4 < 0. \tag{3.52}$$

The ordinary least-squares estimate of equation 3.51 is given by

$$Ci = +10498.24 - 0.00029Pi + 0.73694Di + 0.99240Ii - 987.193Ri$$
$$\quad (+7.54) \quad\quad (-2.71) \quad\quad (+3.97) \quad\quad (+3.41) \quad\quad (-3.33)$$

$$R^2 = 0.63 \quad \langle R \rangle_{av}{}^2 = 0.58 \quad n = 36 \quad DF = 31$$

$$F = 13.0817 \quad \langle C \rangle_{av} i = 15180.54 \tag{3.53}$$

where terms in parentheses are $t$-values.

All four of the coefficients in equation 3.53 have the expected signs. In addition, all four coefficients are statistically significant at well beyond the 0.01 level. The $R^2$ is 0.63, and the $\langle R \rangle_{av}{}^2$ is 0.58, so that the model explains approximately three-fifths of the variation in the cost-of-living variable. The $F$-ratio is statistically significant at far beyond the 0.01 level.

There is only one case of multicollinearity; the zero-order correlation coefficient between the exogenous variables $Pi$ and $Di$ is +0.82. However, since the $t$-values of both of these variables in equation 3.53 are statistically significant at well beyond the 0.01 level, the high degree of correlation between $Pi$ and $Di$ is not of any great concern.

The ordinary least-squares estimate of equation 3.51 excluding Honolulu from the data pool is given by

$$Ci = +11073.34 - 0.00016Pi + 0.54640Di + 0.83311Ii - 897.101Ri$$
$$\quad (+10.58) \quad\quad (-1.90) \quad\quad (+3.80) \quad\quad (+3.80) \quad\quad (-4.03)$$

$$R^2 = 0.71 \quad \langle R \rangle_{av}{}^2 = 0.67 \quad n = 35 \quad DF = 30$$

$$F = 18.5017 \qquad \langle C \rangle_{av} i = 15080.14 \qquad\qquad (3.54)$$

where terms in parentheses are $t$-values.

    All four coefficients in equation 3.54 have the correct signs. Moreover, three of the coefficients (those for variables $Di$, $Ii$, and $Ri$) are statistically significant at beyond the 0.01 level, whereas the coefficient on the remaining variable ($Pi$) is statistically significant at roughly the 0.05 level. The $R^2$ is 0.71, and the $\langle R \rangle_{av}^2$ is 0.67; thus, the model explains approximately 70 percent of the variation in the dependent variable. The $F$-ratio is statistically significant at far beyond the 0.01 level.

    On the basis of the strong performances by all of the independent variables in both regressions 3.53 and 3.54, several conclusions can be derived. For the year 1975, the cost of living in SMSAs was directly related to both population density and per-capita income and inversely related to population size and the presence of right-to-work legislation.

*The Year 1976*

For the year 1976, the following regression equation is to be estimated by ordinary least squares:

$$Ci = m_0 + m_1 Pi + m_2 Di + m_3 Ii + m_4 Ri + \mu_{11} \qquad (3.55)$$

where

    $Ci$ is the average annual cost of living in SMSA $i$ in 1976, for a four-person family living on an intermediate budget;

    $m_0$ is a constant term;

    $Pi$ is the 1976 population in SMSA $i$;

    $Di$ is the population density in SMSA $i$ in 1976, expressed as the number of persons per square mile;

    $Ii$ is the 1976 per-capita income level in SMSA $i$;

    $Ri$ is a dummy variable to indicate the existence of right-to-work laws in 1976 in the state where SMSA $i$ is principally located; and

    $\mu_{11}$ is a stochastic-error term.

Sufficient data were available to permit an analysis of thirty-nine SMSAs. The expected signs on the coefficients in regression equation 3.55 are

$$m_1 < 0, \ m_2 > 0, \ m_3 > 0, \ \text{and} \ m_4 < 0. \quad\quad (3.56)$$

The ordinary least-squares estimate of equation 3.55 is given by

$$Ci = +12529.63 - 0.00023Pi + 0.73506Di + 0.54568Ii - 1105.72Ri$$
$$\quad\quad (+6.82) \quad\quad (-1.68) \quad\quad (+3.17) \quad\quad (+1.97) \quad\quad (-3.06)$$

$$R^2 = 0.53 \quad\quad \langle R \rangle_{av}^2 = 0.48 \quad\quad n = 39 \quad\quad DF = 34$$

$$F = 9.7278 \quad\quad \langle C \rangle_{av} i = 16143.10 \quad\quad\quad\quad\quad\quad\quad (3.57)$$

where terms in parentheses are $t$-values.

In equation 3.57, all four of the coefficients have the expected signs. In addition, two of the coefficients (those for variables $Di$ and $Ri$) are statistically significant at the 0.01 level, whereas a third coefficient (that for variable $Ii$) is statistically significant at the 0.05 level. The coefficient of the population-size variable ($Pi$) is statistically significant at only the 0.10 level. The $R^2$ is 0.53, and the $\langle R \rangle_{av}^2$ is 0.48, so that the model explains roughly half of the variation in the living-cost variable. The $F$-statistic is significant at approximately the 0.01 level.

The zero-order correlation coefficients among the independent variables in equation 3.57 are provided in table 3–8. As indicated in table 3–8, there are two possible multicollinearity problems in the present analysis:

1. $Pi$ and $Ii$, at +0.58; and
2. $Pi$ and $Di$, at +0.82.

The light degree of correlation between $Pi$ and $Ii$, on the one hand, and between $Pi$ and $Di$, on the other hand, very likely accounts for the relative weakness of the coefficient for variable $Pi$ in equation 3.57.[18] Estimating equation 3.55 by ordinary least squares, excluding Honolulu, generates empirical results that are very nearly identical to those in equation 3.57. The following conclusions can be inferred: the cost of living

**Table 3–8**
**Correlation Coefficients, 1976**

|       | $Pi$  | $Di$  | $Ii$  | $Ri$  |
|-------|-------|-------|-------|-------|
| $Pi$  | 1.00  |       |       |       |
| $Di$  | 0.82  | 1.00  |       |       |
| $Ii$  | 0.58  | 0.41  | 1.00  |       |
| $Ri$  | -0.25 | -0.26 | -0.27 | 1.00  |

in SMSAs during 1976 was an increasing function of population density and per-capita income; and the cost of living in SMSAs in 1976 was a decreasing function of population size and the presence of right-to-work legislation.

*The Year 1977*

To investigate empirically the determinants of geographic living-cost differentials for the year 1977, the following regression is postulated:

$$Ci = n_0 + n_1Pi + n_2Di + n_3Ii + n_4Ri + \mu_{12} \qquad (3.58)$$

where

$Ci$ is the average annual cost of living in SMSA $i$ in 1977, for a four-person family living on an intermediate budget;

$n_0$ is a constant term;

$Pi$ is the 1977 population in SMSA $i$;

$Di$ is the population density in SMSA $i$ in 1977, expressed in terms of the number of persons per square mile;

$Ii$ is the per-capita income level in SMSA $i$ in 1977;

$Ri$ is a dummy variable to indicate the existence of right-to-work legislation in 1977 in the state where SMSA $i$ is principally located; and

$\mu_{12}$ is a stochastic-error term.

Because of data limitations for the year 1977, the following four SMSAs were excluded from the empirical analysis: Boston, Mass.; Hartford, Conn.; Portland, Maine; and Durham, N.C. Only thirty-five SMSAs were examined for 1977.

The expected signs on the various linear coefficients in regression equation 3.58 are as follows:

$$n_1 < 0, n_2 > 0, n_3 > 0, \text{ and } n_4 < 0. \qquad (3.59)$$

The ordinary least-squares estimate of equation 3.57 is given by

$$Ci = +12216.72 - 0.00031Pi + 0.89610Di + 0.99326Ii - 1293.93Ri$$
$$(+7.75) \qquad (-2.63) \qquad (+4.40) \qquad (+3.04) \qquad (-4.02)$$

$$R^2 = 0.70 \qquad \langle R \rangle_{av}^2 = 0.66 \qquad n = 35 \qquad DF = 30$$

$$F = 17.8228 \qquad \langle C \rangle_{av}i = 16863.11 \tag{3.60}$$

where terms in parentheses are $t$-values.

In regression estimate 3.60, all four coefficients exhibit the hypothesized signs. In addition, all four coefficients are statistically significant at beyond the 0.01 level. The $R^2$ is 0.70, and the $\langle R \rangle_{av}^2$ is 0.66; the model explains over two-thirds of the variation in the cost-of-living level for the year 1977. The $F$-ratio is statistically significant at far beyond the 0.01 level.

In regression estimate 3.60, there is only one case of multicollinearity, a zero-order correlation coefficient of $+0.81$ between the variables $Pi$ and $Di$. This high degree of correlation between $Pi$ and $Di$ is to be expected and has been encountered thus far in all of the regression estimates in this chapter. For the year 1977, however, the multicollinearity issue is not a matter of great concern since the coefficients of both variables are highly significant in regression equation 3.60.

The ordinary least-squares estimate of equation 3.58 excluding Honolulu is given by

$$Ci = +12838.33 - 0.00016Pi + 0.67346Di + 0.81563Ii - 1191.10Ri$$
$$\phantom{Ci =} (+11.20) \qquad (-1.75) \qquad (+4.40) \qquad (+3.42) \qquad (-5.10)$$

$$R^2 = 0.79 \qquad \langle R \rangle_{av}^2 = 0.77 \qquad n = 34 \qquad DF = 29$$

$$F = 27.8968 \qquad \langle C \rangle_{av}i = 16744.81 \tag{3.61}$$

where terms in parentheses are $t$-values.

As shown in equation 3.61, the exclusion of Honolulu from the data base does alter the regression results somewhat. The most obvious change is the loss of statistical significance of the coefficient for variable $Pi$. The coefficient in question is statistically significant at beyond the 0.01 level in equation 3.60, whereas it is statistically significant at only the 0.08 level in equation 3.61.

On the basis of the findings in equations 3.60 and 3.61, several conclusions can be generated. On the one hand, the cost of living in SMSAs in 1977 was an increasing function of both population density and per-capita income. On the other hand, the cost of living in SMSAs in 1977 was a decreasing function of the presence of right-to-work laws and probably of population size as well.[19]

*The Year 1978*

The investigation of the determinants of geographic living-cost differentials for the year 1978 postulates the following regression equation:[20]

$$Ci = q_0 + q_1 Pi + q_2 Di + q_3 Ii + q_4 Ri + \mu_{13} \qquad (3.62)$$

where

> $Ci$ is the average annual cost of living in SMSA $i$ in 1978, for a four-person family living on an intermediate budget;
>
> $q_0$ is a constant term;
>
> $Pi$ is the total population in SMSA $i$ in 1978;
>
> $Di$ is the population density in SMSA $i$ in 1978, expressed in terms of the number of persons per square mile;
>
> $Ii$ is the per-capita income level in SMSA $i$ in 1977;
>
> $Ri$ is a dummy variable indicating the existence of right-to-work legislation in the state where SMSA $i$ is principally located; and
>
> $\mu_{13}$ is a stochastic-error term.

The hypothesized signs of the linear coefficients in regression equation 3.62 are

$$q_1 < 0, \; q_2 > 0, \; q_3 > 0, \text{ and } q_4 < 0. \qquad (3.63)$$

Sufficient data were available for the year 1978 to study thirty-nine SMSAs. This fact generates thirty-nine sets of data points and hence thirty-four degrees of freedom; the latter number represents the maximum number of degrees of freedom possible within this model using cross-section analysis.

The ordinary least-squares estimate of equation 3.62 is

$$Ci = +13286.81 - 0.00035 Pi + 0.94301 Di + 0.72372 Ii - 1344.50 Ri$$
$$(+6.11) \qquad (-2.28) \qquad (+3.67) \qquad (+2.44) \qquad (-3.16)$$

$$R^2 = 0.54 \qquad \langle R \rangle_{av}^2 = 0.49 \qquad n = 39 \qquad DF = 34$$

$$F = 10.1343 \qquad \langle C \rangle_{av} i = 18543.44 \qquad\qquad (3.64)$$

where terms in parentheses are signed $t$-values.

In regression estimate 3.64, all four coefficients have the expected signs. In addition, all four coefficients are statistically significant at the 0.01 level or beyond. The $R^2$ is 0.54, and the $\langle R \rangle_{av}^2$ is 0.49, so that the model explains approximately half of the variation in the cost-of-living variable. The $F$-statistic is significant at the 0.01 level.

The zero-order correlation coefficients among the independent variables in regression estimate 3.64 are provided in table 3–9. This table reveals two cases of possible multicollinearity. They are

1. $Pi$ and $Ii$, at +0.54; and
2. $Pi$ and $Di$, at +0.77.

The high correlation between $Pi$ and $Di$ is no surprise; furthermore, a high correlation between $Pi$ and $Ii$ has been observed in certain of the earlier regressions in this chapter. Since the coefficients on all three variables in equation 3.64 perform very well, neither of these cases of high correlation should be viewed as a major problem.[21]

The ordinary least-squares estimate of equation 3.62 excluding Honolulu yields results that do not differ materially from those in equation 3.64. As a consequence it can be concluded that for the year 1978, the cost of living in SMSAs was an increasing function of population density and per-capita income and a decreasing function of population size and the existence of right-to-work legislation.

*The Year 1979*

For the year 1979, the regression equation to be estimated is given by

$$Ci = r_0 + r_1 Pi + r_2 Di + r_3 Ii + r_4 Ri + \mu_{14} \qquad\qquad (3.65)$$

**Table 3–9**
**Correlation Coefficients, 1978**

|      | Pi    | Di    | Ii    | Ri   |
|------|-------|-------|-------|------|
| Pi   | 1.00  |       |       |      |
| Di   | 0.77  | 1.00  |       |      |
| Ii   | 0.53  | 0.29  | 1.00  |      |
| Ri   | −0.24 | −0.28 | −0.21 | 1.00 |

where

$C_i$ is the average annual cost of living in SMSA $i$ in 1979, for a four-person family living on an intermediate budget;

$r_0$ is a constant term;

$P_i$ is the total population in SMSA $i$ in 1978;

$D_i$ is the population density in SMSA $i$ in 1978, expressed in terms of the number of persons per square mile;

$I_i$ is the per-capita income level in SMSA $i$ in 1979;

$R_i$ is a dummy variable used to indicate the presence of right-to-work legislation in 1979 in the state where SMSA $i$ is principally located; and

$\mu_{14}$ is a stochastic-error term.

As was the case in the preceding regressions in this chapter, we would expect the following signs on the coefficients in regression equation 3.65:

$$r_1 < 0, \; r_2 > 0, \; r_3 > 0, \; \text{and } r_4 < 0. \tag{3.66}$$

The year 1978 was the last year for which the U.S. Bureau of Labor Statistics compiled geographically comparable living-cost data for as many as thirty-nine SMSAs. In point of fact, for the year 1979, such data are available for only twenty-four SMSAs. The following SMSAs were studied: Atlanta, Ga.; Baltimore, Md.; Boston, Mass.; Buffalo, N.Y.; Chicago, Ill.; Cincinnati, Ohio; Cleveland, Ohio; Dallas, Tex.; Denver, Col.; Detroit, Mich.; Honolulu, Hawaii; Houston, Tex.; Kansas City, Mo.; Los Angeles–Long Beach, Cal.; Milwaukee, Wis.; Minneapolis–St. Paul, Minn.; New York, N.Y.; Philadelphia, Pa.; Pittsburgh, Pa.; St. Louis, Mo.; San Diego, Cal.; San Francisco–Oakland, Cal.; Seattle–Everett, Wash.; and Washington, D.C.

The ordinary least-squares estimate of equation 3.65 is given by

$$C_i = +19936.93 - 0.00046P_i + 1.06703D_i + 0.15633I_i - 1973.33R_i$$
$$\quad (+5.86) \quad\;\; (-2.08) \quad\;\; (+3.00) \quad\;\;\; (+0.44) \quad\;\; (-2.62)$$

$$R^2 = 0.52 \quad \langle R \rangle_{av}^2 = 0.42 \quad n = 24 \quad DF = 19$$

$$F = 5.1216 \quad \langle C \rangle_{av}i = 20974.81 \tag{3.67}$$

where terms in parentheses are $t$-values.

In equation 3.67, all four coefficients have the expected signs. In addition, the coefficients of variables $Di$ and Ri are statistically significant at the 0.01 level, whereas the coefficient of variable $Pi$ is statistically significant at about the 0.05 level. The variable $Ii$, however, is not statistically significant at even the 0.10 level. The $R^2$ is 0.52, and the $\langle R \rangle_{av}{}^2$ is 0.42, so that the model explains roughly half of the variation in the dependent variable. The $F$-ratio is statistically significant at the 0.05 level.

For the exogenous variables in equation 3.67, there is only one case where a high degree of correlation is encountered. The zero-order correlation coefficient between variables $Pi$ and $Di$ is +0.78. This multicollinearity may account for the less-than-impressive performance by variable $Pi$ in equation 3.67.

Estimating equation 3.65 by ordinary least-squares with Honolulu excluded from the analysis yields

$$Ci = +19896.61 - 0.00020Pi + 0.74030Di + 0.09836Ii - 1784.75Ri$$
$$\phantom{Ci = }(+7.54) \quad\;\; (-1.07) \quad\;\; (+2.55) \quad\;\; (+0.36) \quad\;\; (-3.04)$$

$$R^2 = 0.58 \quad \langle R \rangle_{av}{}^2 = 0.48 \quad n = 23 \quad DF = 18$$

$$F = 6.1281 \quad \langle C \rangle_{av}i = 20765.01 \tag{3.68}$$

where terms in parentheses are $t$-values.

Although all four of the estimated coefficients in equation 3.68 have the expected signs, only two (those for variables $Di$ and $Ri$) are statistically significant at acceptable levels.[22] The variables $Pi$ and $Ii$ are not even statistically significant at the 0.15 level.

On the basis of the findings in equations 3.67 and 3.68, we can confidently conclude only the following: the cost of living in SMSAs during 1979 was an increasing function of population density and a decreasing function of the presence of right-to-work laws.

## The Case of Honolulu: A Simple Time-Series Analysis

The regression analyses provided for the years 1966 through 1979 are cross-sectional in nature. The inclusion of Honolulu, Hawaii—a single set of observations—profoundly influences the empirical findings in several of the fourteen regression estimates. This section of the chapter seeks to apply the basic model developed in chapter 2 to the single case of Honolulu. The analysis in question will be time-series in nature. The model to be applied to the Honolulu SMSA is described initially by

$$Ct = s_0 + s_1Pt + s_2Dt + s_3It + s_4Rt + \mu_{15} \qquad (3.69)$$

where

$Ct$ is the average annual cost of living in the Honolulu SMSA in year $t$, for a four-person family living on an intermediate budget;

$s_0$ is a constant term;

$Pt$ is the total population in the Honolulu SMSA in year $t$;

$Dt$ is the population density in the Honolulu SMSA in year $t$, expressed in terms of the number of persons per square mile;

$It$ is the per-capita income level in the Honolulu SMSA in year $t$;

$Rt$ is a dummy variable used to indicate the presence of right-to-work legislation in Hawaii in year $t$; and

$\mu_{15}$ is a stochastic-error term.

Several pertinent observations regarding the model in equation 3.69 are in order. First, in all of the years for which this study is conducted, there were no right-to-work laws in Hawaii. For all values of $t$, it therefore follows that

$$Rt = 0. \qquad (3.70)$$

As a result, the model in equation 3.69 becomes

$$Ct = s_0 + s_1Pt + s_2Dt + s_3It + \mu_{15} \qquad (3.71)$$

Next, the time period for which adequate data are available runs from 1966 through 1979. It follows that

$$t = 1966, \ldots, 1979. \qquad (3.72)$$

From equation 3.72, it follows that there are fourteen observations; from 3.71, it follows that there are four estimators: $s_0$, $s_1$, $s_2$, and $s_3$. Therefore, the total degrees of freedom will be only ten. This very limited number of degrees of freedom requires relatively large $t$-statistics in order to establish statistical significance.

The ordinary least-squares estimate of equation 3.71 is given by

$$Ct = +43240.31 + 0.00036Pt + 0.66149Dt + 4.07176It$$
$$(+6.30) \qquad (+2.07) \qquad (+6.07) \qquad (+13.81)$$

$$R^2 = 0.99 \quad \langle R \rangle_{av}{}^2 \quad n = 14 \quad DF = 10$$

$$F = 662.921 \quad D - W = 2.63 \qquad\qquad (3.73)$$

where terms in parentheses are $t$-values.

The results in equation 3.73 indicate that as per-capita income and population density rose over the period, so too did the cost of living. The population-variable coefficient is not statistically significant at any acceptable (that is, 0.05 or better) significance level. These results in no way alter the basic inferences derived from the preceding fourteen sets of cross-section regression estimates.

**Right-to-Work Laws and Living Costs**

Scrutiny of the cross-sectional findings for the years 1966 through 1979 reveals an extremely consistent and relatively powerful impact of the existence of right-to-work laws on cost of living. Table 3–10 provides the following information for the years 1966 through 1979:

1. the coefficient on the right-to-work law variable, by year;
2. the mean value of the cost of living, by year; and
3. the ratio of the right-to-work-law coefficient to the mean value of cost of living, by year.

**Table 3–10**
**The Impact of Right-to-Work Laws**

| Year | Coefficient | Mean Living Cost | Ratio of Coefficient to Living Cost (decimal) |
|------|-------------|------------------|-----------------------------------------------|
| 1966 | −482.30 | 9221.95 | −0.05 |
| 1967 | −519.89 | 9097.66 | −0.06 |
| 1968 | −557.31 | 9085.95 | −0.06 |
| 1969 | −645.33 | 10063.51 | −0.06 |
| 1970 | −622.95 | 10644.31 | −0.06 |
| 1971 | −647.16 | 10952.24 | −0.06 |
| 1972 | −699.85 | 11372.63 | −0.06 |
| 1973 | −799.04 | 12806.19 | −0.06 |
| 1974 | −824.46 | 14239.71 | −0.06 |
| 1975 | −987.19 | 15180.54 | −0.07 |
| 1976 | −1105.72 | 16143.10 | −0.07 |
| 1977 | −1293.93 | 16863.11 | −0.08 |
| 1978 | −1344.50 | 18543.44 | −0.07 |
| 1979 | −1973.33 | 20974.81 | −0.09 |

Table 3–10 reveals a very consistent pattern, especially through the year 1974, where the following obtains:

$$\partial Ci/\partial Ri \cong -0.06. \tag{3.74}$$

Beginning with the year 1975, there is a pattern in which the apparent impact of right-to-work laws on living costs rises somewhat. The findings summarized in table 3–10 may be invaluable to policymakers at a time when right-to-work laws are still under debate.

## Summary and Conclusions

In all of the cross-sectional estimates presented in this chapter, all four of the estimated coefficients (population size, population density, per-capita income, and right-to-work laws) exhibited the hypothesized signs. In addition, in most of the estimations most of the coefficients in question were statistically significant at the 0.05 level or beyond. Moreover, in several of the estimations, all four coefficients were statistically significant at the 0.01 level or beyond. Accordingly, we infer that rather strong empirical evidence has been generated in support of the four sets of hypotheses developed in chapter 2.

The basic model examined in this chapter is given by

$$Ci = Ci \; (Pi, \; Di, \; Ii, \; Ri) \tag{3.75}$$

where $Ci$, $Pi$, $Di$, $Ii$, $Ri$ are as for equation 3.1.

The empirical findings in this chapter indicate that, in over 90 percent of the estimates, the coefficient on the variable $Pi$ (population size) is statistically significant at the 0.05 level or beyond.[23] All else being equal it follows that

$$\partial Ci/\partial Pi < 0. \tag{3.76}$$

The relationship in equation 3.76 is illustrated in figure 3–1.

The empirical results in the present chapter indicate that, in all fourteen of the regression estimates that include the SMSA of Honolulu, Hawaii, the coefficient on the population-density variable $Di$ is statistically significant at the 0.01 level or beyond. This implies, all else equal, that

$$\partial Ci/\partial Di > 0. \tag{3.77}$$

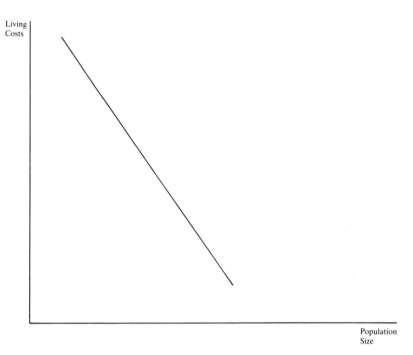

**Figure 3–1.** Population Size and Living Costs

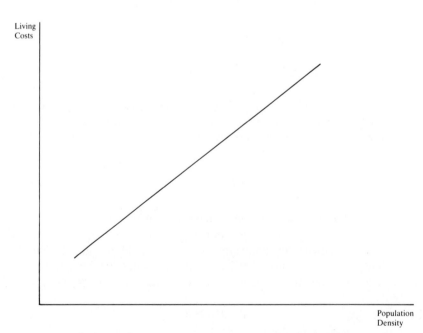

**Figure 3–2.** Population Density and Living Costs

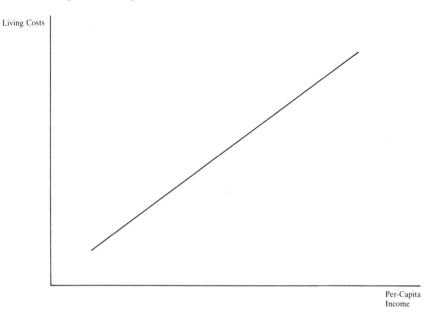

**Figure 3-3.** Per-Capita Income and Living Costs

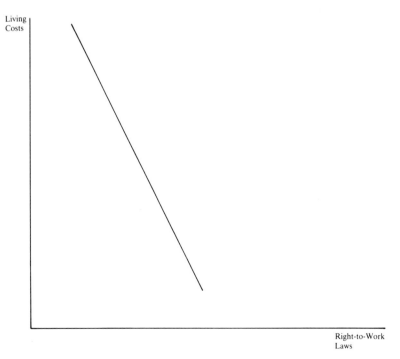

**Figure 3-4.** Right-to-Work Laws and Living Costs

The relationship expressed in equation 3.77 is depicted graphically in figure 3–2.

Examining the empirical findings that include the data for Honolulu reveals that, in approximately 79 percent of the cases, the coefficient on the income variable $Ii$ (per-capita income) is statistically significant at the 0.05 level or beyond. This lends a reasonable amount of empirical support for the hypothesis that:

$$\partial Ci/\partial Ii > 0. \qquad (3.78)$$

This relationship is represented graphically in figure 3–3.

Finally, the empirical findings in this chapter indicate that the coefficient on the right-to-work variable was statistically significant at the 0.01 level or beyond in all fourteen of the regression estimates. Hence we would argue ceteris paribus that

$$\partial Ci/\partial Ri < 0. \qquad (3.79)$$

This relationship is depicted graphically in figure 3–4.

Overall, the population-size, population-density, per-capita-income, and right-to-work-law variables performed extremely well. The basic hypotheses developed in chapter 2 all received strong empirical support. We can conclude that the overall cost of living in metropolitan areas is a direct function of both population density and per-capita income; furthermore, the cost of living in metropolitan areas is an inverse function of both population size and right-to-work legislation.

In the following chapter, alternative specifications of the model are examined in the hope of providing yet better insights into the basic issue of geographic living-cost differentials.

## Notes

1. The dummy variable to be used in this chapter will assume values of either one or zero. A log-linear specification cannot deal with zeros. Related to this, see Goldfeld and Quandt (1972), Johnston (1972), and Judge, Griffiths, Hill, and Lee (1980).

2. It can possibly be argued that $\partial^2 Ci/\partial Di^2 > 0$. Nevertheless, this is an issue that need not absorb space in the current discussion since the principal concern relative to variable $Di$ is in its first partial derivative.

3. One could, of course, argue that this interpretation is arbitrary. In point of act, it may be somewhat arbitrary; nevertheless, it remains to be seen whether the choice involved represents a substantive problem of any sort.

4. Related to this, see the study by Brackett (1973).

5. The use of dummy variables is quite common. See, for example, Gallaway and Cebula (1973) or Cebula (1979).

6. In equation 3.15, all of the variables involved are statistically significant at beyond the 0.01 level.

7. Note the declines, relative to equation 3.15, in the mean of the dependent variable and in the size of the constant term.

8. Once again, observe that either $Ri = 0$ or $Ri = 1$. This condition obtains in all of the remaining regressions involving $Ri$.

9. The estimates being referred to here are for the years 1966 through 1969.

10. These ordinary least-squares results are given by

$$Ci = +8026.91 - 0.00017Pi + 0.50835Di + 0.16527Ii - 617.478Ri$$
$$(+10.78) \quad (-2.79) \quad (+3.62) \quad (+3.31) \quad (-3.75)$$

$$R^2 = 0.73 \quad \langle R \rangle_{av}^2 = 0.69 \quad n = 38 \quad DF = 33$$

$$F = 21.7545 \quad \langle C \rangle_{av}i = 10588.14$$

where terms in parentheses are $t$-values.

11. The $F$-ratio is statistically significant at beyond the 0.01 level.

12. The overall empirical results in equations 3.42 and 3.43 are inferior to those for the earlier years studied.

13. The letter $i$ was skipped over in order to prevent notational difficulties.

14. The population density was determined by dividing the 1973 population by the sum of the 1970 city and county land-area census statistics and the additional land areas added between 1970 and 1973 (these changes affected nearly every SMSA).

15. The population statistic for Hartford, Conn. is for the year 1973.

16. Actually, the coefficients on both $Di$ and $Ri$ are statistically significant in equation 3.50 at the 0.01 level.

17. The $F$-ratio in equation 3.50 is statistically significant at beyond the 0.01 level.

18. The marginal performance by the income variable $Ii$ is also very likely attributable to multicollinearity.

19. The word *probably* is inserted because of the weakness of the coefficient for variable $Pi$ in equation 3.61.

20. To avoid notation problems, the symbols $o$ and $p$ have been skipped over.

21. That is, the variables $Pi$, $Di$, and $Ri$ all perform well in equation 3.64.

22. The minimum acceptable level of statistical significance in this analysis is the 0.05 level.

23. This observation applies solely to those estimates that include Honolulu, Hawaii, in the data base.

**References**

Brackett, J. 1973. "Intercity Differences in Family Food Budget Costs." *Monthly Labor Review* 96:1189–1194.

Cebula, R.J. 1979. *The Determinants of Human Migration*. Lexington, Mass.: D.C. Heath, Lexington Books.

Gallaway, L.E., and Cebula, R.J. 1973. "Differentials and Indeterminacy in Wage-Rate Analysis: An Empirical Note." *Industrial and Labor Relations Review* 26:991–995.

Goldfeld, S.M., and Quandt, R.E. 1972. *Nonlinear Methods in Econometrics*. New York: North-Holland.

Johnston, J. 1972. *Econometric Methods*. New York: McGraw-Hill.

Judge, G.G., Griffiths, W.E., Hill, R.C., and Lee, T. 1980. *The Theory and Practice of Econometrics*. New York: Wiley.

**Part III
Extensions of the Model:
Static and Dynamic**

# 4

# Static Extensions of the Basic Model

The purpose of this chapter is to extend the basic model developed in chapter 2 and examined in chapter 3. The following additional variables will be developed and empirically tested for potential impact on living costs:

1. utility-price differentials;
2. property taxation; and
3. an alternative to the dummy right-to-work variable $(Ri)$ to measure labor-market characteristics and conditions.

In chapter 5, a simple dynamic model will be developed.

## Utility Prices and the Cost of Living

The theoretical model examined in chapter 3 may be described by

$$Ci = Ci \ (Pi, \ Di, \ Ii, \ Ri) \qquad (4.1)$$

where

$Ci$ is a measure of the cost of living in SMSA $i$;

$Pi$ is the total population of SMSA $i$;

$Di$ is the population density in SMSA $i$;

$Ii$ is the per-capita income level in SMSA $i$; and

$Ri$ is an indicator of the presence of right-to-work legislation in SMSA $i$.

This model can be expanded by including a measure of average-unit utility prices. The theoretical argument for this measure is presented, followed by an empirical analysis.

### Theoretical Analysis

It is assumed that utility-price differentials among SMSAs can affect household living expenses in at least two different ways. First, higher utility prices directly increase living costs by adding to the aggregate costs of maintaining any given standard of living.[1] Naturally, the more price-inelastic the demand curve for utilities, the greater the impact of higher utility prices on living costs.[2] Let the price elasticity of demand for a utility be given by

$$\alpha = (-)(A/Q) \cdot (dQ/dA) \tag{4.2}$$

where

α is the price elasticity of demand for the utility;

$A$ is the unit price of the utility;

$Q$ is the number of units of the utility demanded; and

$dQ/dA$ is the slope of the demand curve for the utility.

Now let $Ai$ be the value of $A$ in area $i$. If

$$Ci = Ci\ (Ai, \ \ldots)\ \text{for any}\ i, \tag{4.3}$$

then it follows that

$$[d\ (\partial Ci/\partial Ai)]/d(\alpha i) < 0\ \text{for any}\ i \tag{4.4}$$

where $\alpha i$ is the value of α in area $i$.

Thus, the more price-inelastic the utility-demand curve, the greater the impact of utility-price increases on living costs.

In addition, utility prices can indirectly influence household living costs by influencing the cost structure of firms producing nonutility outputs. In the case of competitive firms, the higher the price of utilities,[3] the higher the average- and marginal-cost curves and hence the higher the unit price required to enable the representative firm to earn precisely zero economic profits.[4] This is illustrated in figure 4–1. The firm initially faces cost curves $AC$ and $MC$. As the price of utilities increases, the cost curves shift upward from $AC$ and $MC$ to $AC^*$ and $MC^*$, respectively. Accordingly, the minimum price required for the generation solely of normal profits for the representative competetive firm rises from $P$ to $P^*$.

The monopolistic case is depicted in figure 4–2. The firm initially maximizes profits at price $P_0$, given cost curves $AC$ and $MC$. With a rise in utility prices, the cost curves shift upward from $AC$ and $MC$ to $AC'$ and $MC'$, respectively. The result is a higher profit-maximizing price, $P'$. Naturally, the degree of upshifting of the cost schedules and hence of the final output

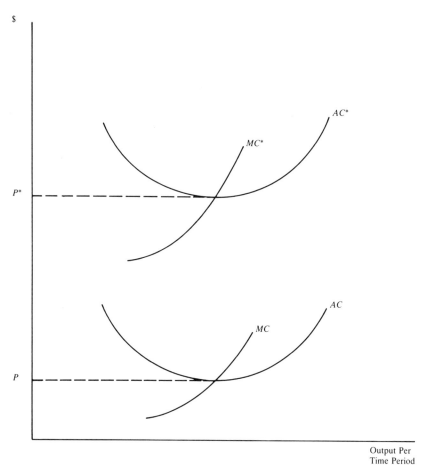

**Figure 4–1.** Utility Prices in a Competitive Market

price depends on the firm's price-elasticity of demand for the utility in question.[5]

Adding the utility variable to the basic model gives a new model:

$$Ci = Ci \, (Pi, \, Di, \, Ii, \, Ri, \, Ai) \qquad (4.5)$$

where $Ci$, $Pi$, $Di$, $Ii$, and $Ri$ are as in equation 4.1; and $Ai$ is the unit price of a given utility in SMSA $i$.

The linear form of equation 4.5 is as follows:

$$Ci = a_0 + a_1 Pi + a_2 Di + a_3 Ii + a_4 Ri + a_5 Ri + \mu \qquad (4.6)$$

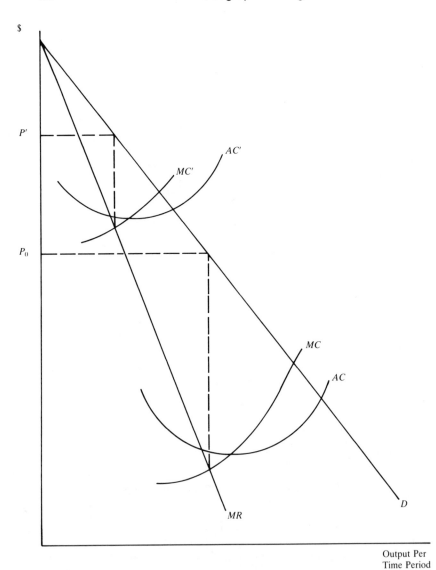

**Figure 4–2.** The Monopolistic Market and Utility Prices

where

  *Ci, Pi, Di, Ii, Ri,* and *Ai* are as in equation 4.1;

  $a_0$ is a constant term; and

  $\mu$ is a stochastic-error term.

The following signs on the coefficients in equation 4.6 are to be expected:

$$\partial Ci/\partial Pi = a_1 < 0 \tag{4.7}$$

$$\partial Ci/\partial Di = a_2 > 0 \tag{4.8}$$

$$\partial Ci/\partial Ii = a_3 > 0 \tag{4.9}$$

$$\partial Ci/\partial Ri = a_4 < 0 \tag{4.10}$$

$$\partial Ci/\partial Ai = a_5 > 0 \tag{4.11}$$

The relationship represented in equation 4.11 is illustrated in figure 4–3. The magnitude of the slope of the line in figure 4–3 depends on a complex of

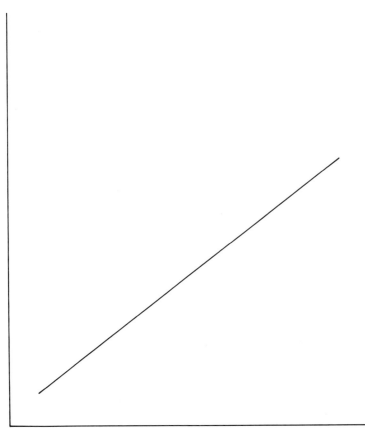

Unit Utility Prices

**Figure 4–3.** Utility Prices and Living Costs

factors; but the concern here is not so much with the quantitative value of the slope of the line as much as with establishing that the line indeed has a positive slope. We will consider the slope of this line in the context of a cross-sectional empirical analysis of equations 4.5 through 4.11.

*Empirical Analysis*

The specific regression equation to be estimated is of the form given by equation 4.6. The new variable in the model, $Ai$, is specifically defined as the "average-unit price of residential heating gas in SMSA $i$."[6] There are available and usable data on the variable $Ai$ for the years 1967 through 1975.[7] The data for variable $Ai$ are available for only twenty SMSAs, however: Atlanta, Ga.; Baltimore, Md.; Boston, Mass.; Buffalo, N.Y.; Chicago, Ill; Cincinnati, Ohio; Cleveland, Ohio; Dallas, Tex.; Detroit, Mich.; Houston, Tex.; Kansas City, Mo.; Milwaukee, Wis.; Minneapolis– St. Paul, Minn.; New York, N.Y.; Philadelphia, Pa.; Pittsburgh, Pa.; St. Louis, Mo.; San Francisco–Oakland, Cal.; Seattle, Wash.; and Washington, D.C. With a set of only twenty observations and a total of six estimators, only fourteen degrees of freedom are possible for the estimations that follow. This situation requires rather high $t$-values in order to establish statistically significant coefficients on the exogenous variables in the regression equations.

   The actual regression equation to be estimated in this section of the chapter is

$$Cit = b_0t + b_1tPit + b_2tDit + b_3tIit + b_4tRit + b_5tAit + \mu t \quad (4.12)$$

where

> $Cit$ is the average annual cost of living in SMSA $i$ during year $t$ for a four-person family living on an intermediate budget;
>
> $b_0t$ is a constant term for year $t$;
>
> $Pit$ is the total population in SMSA $i$ during year $t$;
>
> $Dit$ is the population density in SMSA $i$ during year $t$, expressed in terms of the number of persons per square mile;
>
> $Iit$ is the per-capita income level in SMSA $i$ during year $t$;
>
> $Rit$ is a dummy variable to indicate whether there is right-to-work legislation in the state where SMSA $i$ is principally located, for year $t$;

*Ait* is the average unit price of residential heating gas in SMSA *i* during year *t*; and

$\mu t$ is a stochastic-error term for year *t*.

The values of *t* run as follows: $t = 1967, \ldots, 1975$. Equation 4.12 is to be estimated for each year (for each value of *t*) separately. Thus, no pooling of data and no time-series analysis can be undertaken here. A total of nine estimations will be presented and examined.

The expected signs of the linear coefficients in equation 4.12 are

$$b_1 t < 0, \; b_2 t > 0, \; b_3 t > 0, \; b_4 t < 0, \text{ and } b_5 t > 0. \tag{4.13}$$

where $t = 1967, \ldots, 1975$.

As was the case in chapter 3, the values of the dummy variable are given by

$$Rit = 0 \text{ or } Rit = 1. \tag{4.14}$$

The value for *Rit* is determined in the manner described in the previous chapter following equation 3.30

The ordinary least-squares estimate of regression equation 4.12 for the year 1967 is given by

$$Ci = +6349.08 - 0.00011Pi + 0.25055Di$$
$$(+5.84) \qquad (-1.38) \qquad (+1.45)$$

$$+ \; 0.74847Ii - 589.392Ri + 0.35057Ai$$
$$(+2.49) \qquad (-2.67) \qquad (+1.16)$$

$$R^2 = 0.74 \qquad \langle R \rangle_{av}^2 = 0.65 \qquad n = 20 \qquad DF = 14$$

$$F = 7.98233 \qquad \langle C \rangle_{av} i = 9156.20 \tag{4.15}$$

where terms in parentheses beneath coefficients are signed *t*-values.

In equation 4.15, the signs of the estimated coefficients of all five of the independent variables are as hypothesized. However, only two of the five estimated coefficients are statistically significant at acceptable levels. In particular, the coefficients of both the income and right-to-work-law variables are statistically significant at the 0.01 level. The new variable for utility prices (*Ai*) as well as the population-size (*Pi*) and population-density (*Di*) variables have *t*-values greater than one (in absolute value), but fail in all cases to be statistically significant at even the 0.10 level. The $R^2$ is 0.74, and the $\langle R \rangle_{av}^2 = 0.65$, so that the model explains approximately seven-tenths of the variation in the endogenous variable. The $F$-ratio is statistically significant at the 0.05 level.

The zero-order correlation coefficients among the exogenous variables in equation 4.15 are provided in table 4–1. As shown, the new variable $Ai$ is not in fact unusually correlated with any of the other exogenous variables in the equation. As was observed in all of the estimations in the last chapter, the right-to-work variable also is relatively uncorrelated to the other variables in the analysis. However, the table does reveal the following three cases of multicollinearity:

1. $Ii$ and $Pi$, at $+0.57$;
2. $Ii$ and $Di$, at $+0.58$; and
3. $Pi$ and $Di$, at $+0.93$.

The likely impact of these high degrees of correlation is to dampen the statistical significance of the coefficients of variables $Pi$ and $Di$ in regression estimate 4.15. The $t$-value of the variable $Ii$ in equation 4.15 is high despite the two instances of multicollinearity.

For the year 1968, the ordinary least-squares estimate of equation 4.12 is given by

$$Ci = +6555.47 - 0.00010Pi + 0.26308Di$$
$$(+5.75) \quad (-1.32) \quad (+1.46)$$

$$+ 0.68276Ii - 633.722Ri + 0.52769Ai$$
$$(+2.56) \quad (-2.77) \quad (+1.63)$$

$$R^2 = 0.78 \quad \langle R \rangle_{av}^2 = 0.70 \quad n - 20 \quad DF = 14$$

$$F = 9.73356 \quad \langle C \rangle_{av}i = 9710.25 \quad (4.16)$$

where terms in parentheses are $t$-values.

**Table 4–1**
**Correlation Matrix, 1967, Utility-Price Case**

|      | Pi    | Di    | Ii    | Ri    |      |
|------|-------|-------|-------|-------|------|
| Pi   | 1.00  |       |       |       |      |
| Di   | 0.93  | 1.00  |       |       |      |
| Ii   | 0.57  | 0.58  | 1.00  |       |      |
| Ri   | -0.24 | -0.28 | -0.42 | 1.00  |      |
| Ai   | -0.41 | -0.42 | 0.14  | -0.29 | 1.00 |

In regression estimate 4.16, all five coefficients of the independent variables have the expected signs. The coefficients of variables $Ii$ and $Ri$ are both statistically significant at the 0.01 level, whereas the coefficient of the utility-price variable ($Ai$) is statistically significant at the 0.10 level. The coefficients for variables $Pi$ and $Di$ both fail to be statistically significant at even the 0.10 level. The $R^2$ is 0.78 and the $\langle R \rangle_{av}{}^2$ is 0.70; therefore, the model explains roughly three-fourths of the variation in the cost of living. The $F$-ratio is statistically significant at roughly the 0.01 level.

The multicollinearity problems among the independent variables in equation 4.16 are:

1.   $Ii$ and $Pi$, at +0.55;
2.   $Ii$ and $Di$, at +0.58; and
3.   $Pi$ and $Di$, at +0.93.

These high degrees of correlation very likely are the causes of the weak performances by the variables $Pi$ and $Di$ in regression equation 4.16. Despite the multicollinearity, note that the income variable retains a very high $t$-value in equation 4.16.

For the year 1969, the ordinary least-squares estimate of regression equation 4.12 is given by

$$Ci = +7187.01 - 0.00014Pi + 0.39092Di$$
$$(+5.46) \qquad (-1.82) \qquad (+2.26)$$

$$+ 0.62757Ii - 739.59Ri + 0.47053Ai$$
$$(+2.11) \qquad (-3.06) \qquad (+1.35)$$

$$R^2 = 0.79 \qquad \langle R \rangle_{av}{}^2 = 0.71 \qquad n = 20 \qquad DF = 14$$

$$F = 10.4838 \qquad \langle C \rangle_{av}i = 10259.21 \tag{4.17}$$

where terms in parentheses are $t$-values.

In regression estimate 4.17, the coefficients of all five variables have the expected signs. In addition, one coefficient (that for the right-to-work-law variable $Ri$) is statistically significant at the 0.01 level; two coefficients (those for the variables $Di$ and $Ii$) are statistically significant at the 0.05 level; and one coefficient (that corresponding to the variable $Pi$) is statistically significant at approximately the 0.06 level. Only the coefficient of the utility-price variable ($Ai$) fails to be significant at or near an acceptable level.[8] The explanatory power of the model for the year 1969 is quite high. Since the $R^2$ is 0.79 and the $\langle R \rangle_{av}{}^2$ is 0.71, the model explains a robust three-fourths of the variation in the cost-of-living variable. The $F$-ratio is statistically significant at beyond the 0.01 level.

There are three cases of multicollinearity among the independent variables in equation 4.17:

1.  $Ii$ and $Pi$, at $+0.61$;
2.  $Ii$ and $Di$, at $+0.60$; and
3.  $Pi$ and $Di$, at $+0.91$.

The high degree of correlation in these three cases contributes to the rather weak performances by the involved variables in regression equation 4.17. Nevertheless, it is remarkable that the $t$-values for these three variables turn out to be as high as they do.

The ordinary least-squares estimate of equation 4.12 for the year 1970 is

$$Ci = +7719.91 - 0.00013Pi + 0.41765Di$$
$$(+5.47) \qquad (-1.83) \qquad (+2.62)$$

$$+ 0.55841Ii - 816.487Ri + 0.52443Ai$$
$$(+1.90) \qquad (-3.21) \qquad (+1.43)$$

$$R^2 = 0.81 \qquad \langle R \rangle_{av}^2 = 0.74 \qquad n = 20 \qquad DF = 14$$

$$F = 11.9021 \qquad \langle C \rangle_{av}i = 10818.44 \qquad\qquad (4.18)$$

where terms in parentheses are $t$-values.

In equation 4.18, all five of the estimated coefficients have the expected signs. In addition, two coefficients (for the variables $Di$ and $Ri$) are statistically significant at the 0.01 level or beyond; one coefficient (for the variable $Ii$) is statistically significant at nearly the 0.05 level; and one coefficient (for the variable $Pi$) is statistically significant at approximately the 0.06 level. Only the coefficient of variable $Ai$ fails to be statistically significant at even the 0.10 level. The $R^2$ is 0.81 and the $\langle R \rangle_{av}^2$ is 0.74, so that the model explains roughly four-fifths of the variation in the endogenous variable.[9] The $F$-ratio is statistically significant at beyond the 0.01 level; this fact attests to the overall strength of the model.

Once again, there are three cases of multicollinearity in the zero-order correlation:

1.  $Ii$ and $Pi$, at $+0.60$;
2.  $Ii$ and $Di$, at $+0.58$; and
3.  $Pi$ and $Di$, at $+0.88$.

Although these high degrees of correlation have unquestionably lowered

$t$-values in regression 4.18, the concern here is less than in the preceding three estimates because of the remarkable resiliency of the involved coefficients in the regression equation in question.[10]

The ordinary least-squares estimate of regression equation 4.12 for the year 1971 is

$$Ci = +8921.38 - 0.00015Pi + 0.46427Di$$
$$(+6.11) \qquad (-1.77) \qquad (+2.93)$$

$$+ 0.26997Ii - 918.905Ri + 0.84565Ai$$
$$(+0.97) \qquad (-3.54) \qquad (+2.11)$$

$$R^2 = 0.83 \qquad \langle R \rangle_{av}^2 = 0.76 \qquad n = 20 \qquad DF = 14$$

$$F = 13.2856 \qquad \langle C \rangle_{av}i = 11136.80 \tag{4.19}$$

where terms in parentheses are $t$-values.

All five of the coefficients in regression estimate 4.19 have the correct signs. The coefficients on variables $Di$ and $Ri$ are statistically significant at beyond the 0.01 level, whereas the coefficient on variable $Ai$ is statistically significant at the 0.05 level. This regression is the first in which the utility-price variable exhibits an acceptable level of statistical significance. The population-size variable $Pi$ is merely significant at around the 0.07 level; the per-capita income variable $Ii$, on the other hand, is not statistically significant at even the 0.10 level. With an $R^2$ of 0.83 and an $\langle R \rangle_{av}^2$ of 0.76, the model explains roughly four-fifths of the variation in the living-cost variable. The $F$-ratio is statistically significant at well beyond the 0.01 level.

The following three cases of multicollinearity among the exogenous variables in equation estimate 4.19 were encountered:

1. $Ii$ and $Pi$, at +0.58;
2. $Ii$ and $Di$, at +0.53; and
3. $Pi$ and $Di$, at +0.89.

The first two of these cases of multicollinearity account in part for the poor performance of the income variable in equation 4.19. Similarly, multicollinearity also accounts in part for the statistical weakness of the variable $Pi$ in the regression equation.

The ordinary least-squares estimate of equation 4.12 for the year 1972 is as follows:

$$Ci = +8632.87 - 0.00015Pi + 0.42823Di$$
$$(+5.30) \qquad (-1.44) \qquad (+2.68)$$

$$+ 0.42982Ii - 745.085Ri + 0.66723Ai$$
$$(+1.46) \qquad (-2.19) \qquad (+1.64)$$

$$R^2 = 0.80 \qquad \langle R \rangle_{av}^2 = 0.73 \qquad n = 20 \qquad DF = 14$$

$$F = 11.3624 \qquad \langle C \rangle_{av}i = 11618.03 \tag{4.20}$$

where terms in parentheses are $t$-values.

As usual, all five of the estimated coefficients have the hypothesized signs. In addition, the coefficient of the population-density variable $Di$ is statistically significant at the 0.01 level, and the coefficient of the right-to-work variable $Ri$ is statistically significant at beyond the 0.05 level. The remaining three coefficients, however, are not statistically significant at an acceptable level.[11] The $R^2$ is 0.80 and the $\langle R \rangle_{av}^2$ is 0.73, so that the model explains approximately three-fourths of the variation in the dependent variable. The $F$-ratio is statistically significant at the 0.01 level.

The multicollinearity problems among the independent variables in regression equation 4.20 are somewhat different from those encountered in the earlier regressions in this chapter. The problem cases here are

1. $Ii$ and $Pi$, at $+0.57$;
2. $Ii$ and $Ri$, at $+0.51$; and
3. $Pi$ and $Di$, at $+0.87$.

In the second instance, the right-to-work variable is involved—for the very first time—in multicollinearity. To be sure, this fact in part accounts for the low $t$-value of the income variable $Ii$ in equation 4.20. The first and third instances of multicollinearity undoubtedly contribute to the weakness of the population-size variable in the estimated equation. In addition, the second case of multicollinearity contributes to the observed weakness of the income variable in equation 4.20.

The ordinary least-squares estimate of equation 4.12 for the year 1973 is

$$Ci = +9419.51 - 0.00017Pi + 0.40978Di$$
$$(+5.65) \qquad (-1.64) \qquad (+2.81)$$

$$+ 0.48206Ii - 965.761Ri + 0.92624Ai$$
$$(+1.66) \qquad (-3.07) \qquad (+2.23)$$

$$R^2 = 0.83 \qquad \langle R \rangle_{av}^2 = 0.77 \qquad n = 20 \qquad DF = 14$$

$$F = 13.7067 \qquad \langle C \rangle_{av}i = 13074.02 \tag{4.21}$$

where the terms in parentheses are $t$-values.

For the year 1973, all five of the estimated coefficients have the expected signs. The population-density and right-to-work-law variables are both statistically significant at the 0.01 level. The utility-price variable is statistically significant at roughly the 0.03 level; this finding provides the strongest support thus far for arguing that utility-price differentials influence geographic living-cost differentials. This finding coincides in time with the oil embargo of 1973. As the next two regression estimates help to illustrate, subsequent to 1973 and coincidental with the soaring of fuel prices, there is a dramatic rise in the impact of utility-price (fuel-price) differentials on living-cost differentials. As for the variables $Pi$ and $Ii$, both were statistically significant at only the 0.10 level. The $R^2$ is 0.83 and the $\langle R \rangle_{av}^2$ is 0.77, so that the model explains roughly four-fifths of the variation in the living-cost variable. The $F$-statistic is significant at well beyond the 0.01 level; this attests to the overall strength of the model.

For the independent variables in equation 4.21, multicollinearity was found between

1.  $Ii$ and $Pi$, at $+0.58$;
2.  $Pi$ and $Di$, at $+0.85$;
3.  $Di$ and $Ai$, at $+0.53$.

The first two of these three cases of multicollinearity presumably contribute to the weakness of the variables $Pi$ and $Ii$ in the regression. The high degree of correlation between $Di$ and $Ai$ is of relatively little concern in view of the high $t$-values of both of these variables in regression estimate 4.21.

The ordinary least-squares estimate of regression equation 4.12 for the year 1974 is given by

$$Ci = +11468.81 - 0.00009Pi + 0.35776Di$$
$$(+8.15) \qquad (-0.85) \qquad (+2.20)$$

$$+ 0.30681Ii - 1169.49Ri + 1.16829Ai$$
$$(+1.17) \qquad (-3.58) \qquad (+3.09)$$

$$R^2 = 0.84 \qquad \langle R \rangle_{av}^2 = 0.78 \qquad n = 20 \qquad DF = 14$$

$$F = 14.4142 \qquad \langle C \rangle_{av}i = 14530.03 \qquad\qquad (4.22)$$

where terms in parentheses are $t$-values.

In regression estimate 4.22, the coefficients of all five of the exogenous variables have the expected signs. Two of the variables, $Pi$ and $Ii$, fail to be statistically significant at even the 0.10 level; in fact, the $t$-values of the coefficients for $Pi$ and $Ii$ are even lower in this regression than in the regression for 1973. The coefficient of the population-density variable $Di$ is statistically significant at beyond the 0.05 level; hence, this variable once again seems to have a measurable impact on living costs. The right-to-work-law variable is statistically significant at beyond the 0.01 level, and the utility-price (fuel-price) variable is statistically significant at the 0.01 level. The latter finding is the most convincing evidence so far that utility- (fuel-) cost differentials are significant contributors to geographic living-cost differentials in the United States. The $R^2$ in equation 4.22 is 0.84 and the $\langle R \rangle_{av}^2$ is 0.78; therefore, the model explains approximately four-fifths of the variation in the dependent cost-of-living variable. The $F$-ratio in equation 4.22 is statistically significant at well beyond the 0.01 level.

The only cases of multicollinearity among the exogenous variables in equation 4.22 were between $Pi$ and $Di$, at $+0.86$; and between $Ai$ and $Di$, at $+0.53$. The first of these two cases of high correlation may account, at least in part, for the weakness of the variable $Pi$ in equation 4.22. In view of the resilience of both the variables $Di$ and $Ai$ in regression estimate 4.22, the second case of multicollinearity is of comparatively little concern.[12]

Estimating equation 4.12 by ordinary least squares for the year 1975 yields

$$Ci = +11839.81 - 0.00006Pi + 0.28874Di$$
$$(+5.81) \qquad (-0.42) \qquad (+1.34)$$

$$+ 0.32281Ii - 1035.77Ri + 1.06921Ai$$
$$(+1.02) \qquad (-2.36) \qquad (+2.60)$$

$$R^2 = 0.74 \qquad \langle R \rangle_{av}^2 = 0.64 \qquad n = 20 \qquad DF = 14$$

$$F = 7.81893 \qquad \langle C \rangle_{av} i = 15536.01 \tag{4.23}$$

where terms in parentheses beneath coefficients are signed $t$-values.

As has been true for all of the other estimations in this section of the chapter, the signs of the estimated coefficients for all five of the independent variables in equation 4.23 are as hypothesized. The coefficients of variables $Pi$ and $Ii$ are even weaker in the present regression than in regression 4.22; in any event, in both regressions the variables $Pi$ and $Ii$ fail to achieve statistical significance at even the 0.10 level.[13] In contrast to several of the earlier estimations, the population-density variable in regression estimate 4.23 is not statistically significant at even the 0.10 level. However, the right-to-work variable is statistically significant at roughly the 0.025 level. Next, as was true in equation 4.22, the utility-price (fuel-price) variable is statistically significant at the 0.01 level. Once again, after 1972, utility-price differentials appear to contribute in a very significant fashion to geographic living-cost differentials. In equation 4.23, the $R^2$ is 0.74 and the $\langle R \rangle_{av}^2$ is 0.64. Thus, the model explains roughly two-thirds to seven-tenths of the variation in the dependent living-cost variable. The $F$-ratio in equation 4.23 is statistically significant at the 0.05 level.

There are two cases of multicollinearity among the exogenous variables in regression estimate 4.23: between $Pi$ and $Di,$ at $+0.86$; and between $Ai$ and $Di,$ at $+0.50$. These are the same cases that were encountered in regression 4.22, although there is a slight variation in the magnitudes of the corresponding zero-order correlation coefficients. Both of these particular cases of multicollinearity contribute to a weakened coefficient of the population-density variable $(Di)$. Moreover, the first case of multicollinearity also contributes to a weakened coefficient of the population-size variable. The second case of multicollinearity very likely also has diminished the $t$-value on the coefficient for the utility-price variable. Nevertheless, the $t$-value of variable $Ai$ is sufficiently high that this dimension of multicollinearity is not of any great concern.

The empirical findings presented in this chapter so far cover the time period from 1967 through 1975. In all, forty-five coefficients are estimated, and in all forty-five cases, the coefficients exhibit the expected signs.

Although the population-size variable often exhibits a $t$-value in the range of 1.7 to 1.8, the coefficient of this variable always fails to be statistically significant at the 0.05 level. On the other hand, the $Pi$ variable is statistically significant at the 0.10 level in most cases. These findings are in sharp contrast to the findings in chapter 3.

The population-density variable $Di$ is statistically significant at the 0.05 level or better in two-thirds of the regressions. In point of fact, it is statistically significant at the 0.01 level in four out of the nine cases. Overall, it can be inferred that population density is a comparatively important determinant of living costs in SMSAs. These findings are similar to those in chapter 3.

The per-capita income variable is statistically significant at the 0.05 level in four out of the nine cases. This finding provides only modest support for the hypothesis that living-cost levels are directly related to per-capita income levels. By contrast, chapter 3 provided strong empirical support for the impact of per-capita income on living costs.

The right-to-work-law variable is statistically significant at the 0.05 level or better in all nine cases. In fact, the coefficient on the variable $Ri$ is statistically significant at the 0.01 level in seven out of the nine cases. This variable unquestionably is the most consistent component of the present model. On the basis of these findings, we would rather confidently conclude that right-to-work legislation exercises an extremely important influence over regional living costs in the United States. This conclusion is entirely consistent with the findings in chapter 3.

Finally, the new variable in the model, utility prices, must be considered. In four out of the nine cases, the coefficient of $Ai$ is statistically significant at the 0.05 level; in two out of the nine cases, the coefficient of the variable $Ai$ is statistically significant at the 0.01 level. Prior to 1971, this variable is not statistically significant at an acceptable level; however, except for 1972, it is a significant living-cost determinant for the post–1971 period. By and large, this rise in the statistically significant of variable $Ai$ coincides with the ascent of OPEC power and the concomitant soaring of prices of crude oil and other fuel.[14]

Overall, the model with the addition of the utility-price variable does not perform any better than that developed in chapters 2 and 3. In certain years, the two models perform essentially on a par; for most years, however, the original model is far superior to the present model in terms of generating statistically significant results.

## Property Taxes and Living Costs

In this section of the chapter, the model generated in chapters 2 and 3 is extended with a variable to assess the potential impact of property taxation on geographic living-cost differentials. This investigation will involve both the development of a theoretical argument and the testing of an empirical (regression) model.[15]

### Theoretical Analysis

The existence of large geographic property-tax differentials has been noted by a number of authors, including Cebula (1979), Herber (1971), Maxwell (1969), and Netzer (1966). Typically, as observed by Herber (1971, p. 223), the "property tax tends to have a fairly narrowly classified base." Stated somewhat differently, it is observed by Netzer (1966, pp. 87–88) that the "property tax is largely a tax on investment in land and buildings." Insofar as the property tax is principally a levy against land and buildings, it potentially influences the overall cost of living both directly and indirectly. The cost of living is affected *directly* by property taxes insofar as consumers have to pay property taxes on either the property they own or the property they rent. The cost of living is *indirectly* affected by property taxes when such taxes raise the total costs of production and ultimately the final output prices in the marketplace.

The individual consumer faces a utility function such as

$$U = U(X_1, \ldots, X_n, G_1, \ldots, G_m) \qquad (4.24)$$

where

$U$ is the individual's utility level;

$X_a$ is the individual's consumption of pure private good $a$; $a = 1, \ldots,$ $n$; and

$G_j$ is the individual's consumption of public good $j$; $j = 1, \ldots, m$.[16]

The total cost, $c$, of all of these commodities to the individual is given by

$$C = \sum_{a=1}^{n} P_a X_a + T \qquad (4.25)$$

where $P_a$ is the unit price of commodity $a$; $a = 1, \ldots n$;[17] and $T$ is the individual's total tax bill.

The components of $T$ include income taxation, social-security taxation, sales taxation, and, of course, property taxation. It follows that, all else equal, as the magnitude of property-tax liabilities increases, so too does the magnitude of total tax liabilities. Of course, *all* persons or family units pay property taxes. For homeowners, on the one hand, the liability is clear and entirely direct, despite the very favorable treatment of property taxation in the U.S. Internal Revenue Code.[18] On the other hand, for renters, property tax is included in their gross rental, that is, it is technically added to the net rental fee. Whether this property-tax liability is completely absorbed by the renter or whether it is only partially absorbed by the renter depends on the tightness of the rental-housing market and institutional considerations.[19] In any event, it is clear that *all* family units, as a pragmatic matter, are liable for some property-tax burden.

The higher the property tax, the higher the cost of living:

$$\partial C / \partial TPr > 0 \qquad (4.26)$$

where $TPr$ is the property-tax liability.[20]

In the long run, businesses view the property tax as a form of variable cost. As such, it is a cost that can be avoided entirely only if a firm disappears from the market.[21] Obviously, then, a firm cannot readily avoid the property tax if it chooses to continue (undertake) production. Going further, a firm tends to incur greater property-tax-liability levels if it undertakes greater expansion of its plant and equipment. Since the property tax is principally a tax on capital, the property tax raises the relative price of capital vis-à-vis other productive factors such as labor. At the margin, this change in relative factor prices encourages substitution of labor for capital, that is, the altered factor-price ratio tends to generate a lower capital-to-labor ratio in the actual production process.

Consider the following constrained cost-minimization process. A firm seeks to minimize its total production costs, $L$:

$$L = \sum_{b=1}^{r} P_b F_b \qquad (4.27)$$

where $P_b$ is the unit price of input $b$; $b = 1, \ldots, r$; and $F_b$ is the number of units employed of input $b$; $b = 1, \ldots, r$;

subject to the following output constraint:

$$\langle Q \rangle = Q (F_1, \ldots, F_r) \qquad (4.28)$$

where $Q$ is the number of units of output produced per time period; and $\langle Q \rangle$ is a given value of $Q$.

Figure 4–4 depicts cost minimization for the case where $b = 2$ and $Q = \langle Q \rangle$. The cost of producing $\langle Q \rangle$ units of output per time period is $L_0$ dollars. If a tax on input $F_1$ is imposed, the unit price of the input rises from $P_1$ to

$$P_1 + \Delta P_1 \qquad (4.29)$$

where $\Delta P_1$ is the change in the gross unit price of input $F_1$ as a result of the unit tax on the input. In figure 4–4, the isocost line rotates along the abscissa toward the origin, and the total cost of producing $\langle Q \rangle$ units of output rises above the value $L_0$ to the value $L'$. Given the steeper isocost line, the new minimum cost of producing $\langle Q \rangle$ units of output involves a lower ratio of $F_1$ to $F_2$. In other words it is argued here that

$$[d(F_1/F_2)]/d(\Delta P_1) < 0. \qquad (4.30)$$

On the basis of equation 4.30, we may infer that the higher the property tax, the lower the capital-to-labor ratio. In turn, a lower capital-to-labor ratio implies a more labor-intensive production process. Since the latter process is typically not so amenable to the scale economies that a capital-intensive production process is, the property tax indirectly leads to inefficiencies and higher costs than would otherwise be experienced.

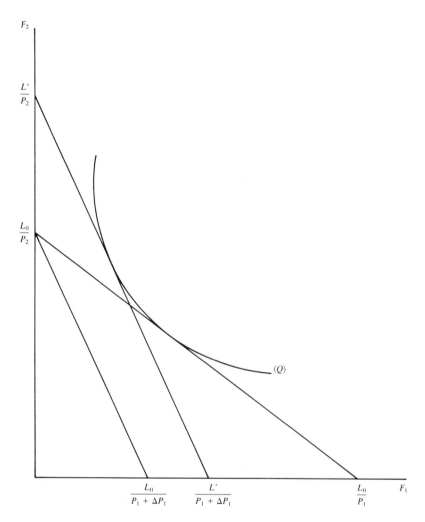

**Figure 4–4.** Constrained Cost Minimization and the Property Tax

Aside from the lower capital-to-labor ratio that property taxation tends to generate, the property tax itself is a component of a firm's total cost structure. Clearly, the higher the firm's property tax, the higher its total costs of production. Thus, the property tax acts directly through total costs *and* through changes in the capital-to-labor ratio to elevate the firm's cost curves. The extent to which property taxes create higher prices, of course, depends upon the degree to which the tax burden can be shifted.[22]

Figure 4–5 illustrates the potential output-price effects of property taxation in a competitive market. The representative firm is initially in long-run equilibrium at point A, where the unit price is given by $P_0$. As a

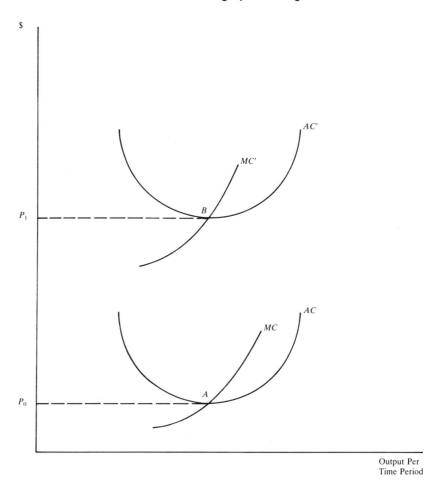

**Figure 4–5.** Property Taxation in a Competitive Market

property tax is imposed, the long-run average- and marginal-cost curves shift upward from $AC$ and $MC$ to $AC'$ and $MC'$, respectively. The new long-run equilibrium is at point B, where the unit price is given by $P_1$. Clearly, $P_1 > P_0$, and the tax is shifted completely (in the long run).

Figure 4–6 illustrates the potential price effects of property taxation in a monopolistic market. A firm is initially in long-run equilibrium at price $P^*$. The imposition of the property tax shifts the cost curves $MC^*$ and $AC^*$ upward to $MC^{**}$ and $AC^{**}$, respectively. The new output price is given by $P^{**}$. Since economic profits are reduced as a result of the tax, the price increase from $P^*$ to $P^{**}$ is associated with only an incomplete shifting of the

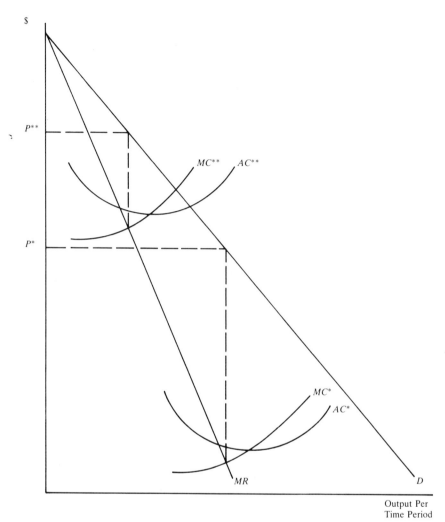

**Figure 4–6.** Property Taxation in a Monopolistic Market

tax. Nevertheless, it is clear that the property tax does act to elevate output prices to the marketplace to at least some extent. The more nearly complete the shifting process, the higher the final-output-price structure will be.

Thus, the property tax both directly and indirectly may influence the overall cost of living. If the property tax is added to the basic model developed in the second and third chapters of this book, the resulting model is given by

$$Ci = Ci\ (Pi,\ Di,\ Ii,\ Ri,\ Ti) \tag{4.31}$$

where $Ci$, $Pi$, $Di$, $Ii$, and $Ri$ are the same as in equation 4.1; and $Ti$ is the per-capita property-tax level in area $i$.

From our analysis it follows that

$$\partial Ci / \partial Ti > 0. \tag{4.32}$$

This hypothesis will be empirically investigated.[23]

*Empirical Analysis of the Property-Tax Variable*

On the basis of equation 4.31, the following regression equation is to be estimated by ordinary least squares:

$$Cit = d_0t + d_1tPit + d_2tDit + d_3tIit + d_4tRit + d_5tTit + \mu t \tag{4.33}$$

where

> $Cit$ is the average annual cost of living in SMSA $i$ during year $t$, for a four-person family living on an intermediate budget;
>
> $d_0t$ is a constant term for year $t$;
>
> $Pit$ is the total population in SMSA $i$ during year $t$;
>
> $Dit$ is the population density in SMSA $i$ during year $t$, expressed in terms of the number of persons per square mile;
>
> $Iit$ is the per-capita income level in SMSA $i$ during the year $t$;
>
> $Rit$ is a dummy variable to indicate the presence of right-to-work legislation in year $t$ in the state in which SMSA $i$ is principally located;
>
> $Tit$ is the per-capita property-tax level in SMSA $i$ during year $t$; and
>
> $\mu t$ is a stochastic-error term for year $t$.

The years for which regression equation 4.33 is to be estimated are 1974, 1975, and 1978. These three years were chosen at random. Given limited data availability for two of these three years, the number of observations is less than thirty-nine except for the year 1975.

The expected signs on the linear coefficients in regression equation 4.33 are

$$d_1 t < 0, \ d_2 t > 0, \ d_3 t > 0, \ d_4 t < 0, \ \text{and} \ d_5 t > 0, \ \text{for all} \ t \quad (4.34)$$

where $t$ = 1974, 1975, and 1978.

The ordinary least-squares estimate of equation 4.33 for the year 1974 is as follows:[24]

$$Ci = +8270.10 - 0.00029Pi + 0.63458Di$$
$$(+6.87) \qquad (-3.62) \qquad (+4.64)$$

$$+ \ 1.14743Ii - 682.855Ri - 0.06594Ti$$
$$(+4.82) \qquad (-2.81) \qquad (-0.63)$$

$$R^2 = 0.80 \qquad \langle R \rangle_{av}^2 = 0.71 \qquad n = 34 \qquad DF = 28$$

$$F = 21.80718 \qquad \langle C \rangle_{av} i = 14531.07 \qquad\qquad (4.35)$$

where terms in parentheses are $t$-values.

Except for the property-tax variable, all of the estimated coefficients for the year 1974 have the expected signs. In addition, the coefficients of the variables $Pi$, $Di$, $Ii$, and $Ri$ are all statistically significant at the 0.01 level. Thus, when the property-tax variable is included in the model, the four basic variables examined in chapters 2 and 3 all perform very well. However, the property-tax variable itself was not statistically significant at any acceptable level. Nevertheless, the present estimate is stronger in nearly every respect than the estimate in equation 4.22, in which the utility-price variable is empirically examined for the same year (1974).

The zero-order correlation coefficients among the independent variables in equation 4.35 are provided in table 4–2. The cases of multicollinearity are

**Table 4–2**
**Correlation Matrix, 1974, Property-Tax Case**

|     | $Pi$  | $Di$  | $Ii$  | $Ri$  |      |
| --- | ----- | ----- | ----- | ----- | ---- |
| $Pi$ | 1.00  |       |       |       |      |
| $Di$ | 0.81  | 1.00  |       |       |      |
| $Ii$ | 0.56  | 0.54  | 1.00  |       |      |
| $Ri$ | -0.29 | -0.32 | -0.41 | 1.00  |      |
| $Ai$ | 0.81  | 0.23  | 0.53  | -0.13 | 1.00 |

1. *Di* and *Pi*, at +0.81;
2. *Di* and *Ii*, at +0.54;
3. *Pi* and *Ii*, at +0.56;
4. *Pi* and *Ti*, at +0.81; and
5. *Ii* and *Ti*, at +0.53.

The last two cases of multicollinearity undoubtedly contribute to the extreme weakness of the property-tax variable in regression estimate 4.35. Despite the first three of these cases of multicollinearity, the coefficients of the involved variables (*Pi, Di,* and *Ii*) were all highly significant in equation 4.35.

The ordinary least-squares estimate of equation 4.33 for the year 1975 is

$$Ci = +12155.62 - 0.00022Pi + 0.62740Di$$
$$(+7.74) \qquad (-1.81) \qquad (+2.99)$$

$$+ \ 0.60540Ii - 1064.94Ri + 1.53317Ti$$
$$(+1.84) \qquad (-3.01) \qquad (+0.69)$$

$$R^2 = 0.56 \qquad \langle R \rangle_{av}^{\ 2} = 0.49 \qquad n = 39 \qquad DF = 33$$

$$F = 8.37929 \qquad \langle C \rangle_{av}i = 15253.14 \tag{4.36}$$

where terms in parentheses are *t*-values.

In equation 4.36, all five of the exogenous variables have the anticipated signs. The population-density and right-to-work-law variables are both statistically significant at beyond the 0.01 level. The population-size and per-capita-income-level variables are statistically significant at roughly the 0.06 level. The property-tax variable, however, fails to be statistically significant at even the 0.15 level. Overall, despite the poor performance by the tax variable, equation 4.36 yields stronger empirical results than does equation 4.23.

The only cases of multicollinearity among the variables in regression equation 4.36 are *Pi* and *Di*, at +0.81; and *Ri* and *Ti*, at +0.52. The first case of multicollinearity certainly comes as no surprise. The second case in part helps to explain the statistical weakness of the property-tax variable in the regression.

For the year 1978, the ordinary least-squares estimate of equation 4.33 is given by[25]

$$Ci = +17211.13 - 0.00028Pi + 0.89119Di$$
$$(+15.21) \qquad (-1.74) \qquad (+2.97)$$

$$+ 0.23652Ii - 14661.10Ri + 1.18878Ti$$
$$(+1.07) \qquad (-3.24) \qquad (+0.56)$$

$$R^2 = 0.50 \qquad \langle R \rangle_{av}^2 = 0.46 \qquad n = 38 \qquad DF = 32$$

$$F = 6.28858 \qquad \langle C \rangle_{av}i = 18543.42 \tag{4.37}$$

where terms in parentheses are $t$-values.

All five of the estimated coefficients in equation 4.37 have the hypothesized signs. Only two coefficients, those for variables $Di$ and $Ri$, are statistically significant at the 0.01 level. None of the remaining coefficients is statistically significant at any acceptable level. Thus, the property-tax variable once again turns out to be an inconsequential determinant of geographic living-cost differentials in the United States.

There are three cases of multicollinearity among the independent variables in equation 4.37:

1. $Pi$ and $Di$, at +0.81;
2. $Pi$ and $Ti$, at +0.50; and
3. $Ii$ and $Ti$, at +0.51.

The last two instances of multicollinearity would certainly account at least in part for the low $t$-value of the property-tax variable in the regression estimate. The first two cases of multicollinearity very likely account for some of the weakness of the population-size coefficient in the regression.

In all three regressions for the years 1974, 1975, and 1978, the estimated coefficient of the property-tax variable fails to be statistically significant at even the 0.15 level. Regression equation 4.33 has also been estimated for several other years; the overall conclusion of those regression estimates is the same as that for the years 1974, 1975, and 1978. To be sure, the weakness on the part of the property-tax variable is largely because of multicollinearity problems. Nevertheless, the consistent weakness of the property-tax coefficient leads to the conclusion that property-tax differentials do not have an important impact on either geographic living-cost levels or geographic living-cost differentials in the United States.

## An Alternative to the Right-to-Work-Law Variable

In all of the living-cost regressions estimated up to this point in the book, the variable $Ri$ has been included as an explanatory variable. This variable has been used to measure the living-cost effects of actual and potential labor-union strength and influence. In this section of the chapter, an alternative to $Ri$ is considered. In particular, this section of the chapter examines the impact on living-cost of a variable measuring the actual percentage of the civilian labor force that is unionized. After a brief theoretical argument is presented, an empirical analysis is provided.

*Theoretical Argument*

Presumably, the larger the extent to which an area's civilian labor force is unionized, the greater the degree of union influence in that area. With greater union influence, the wage package—wages plus fringe benefits— tends to be higher. With a larger wage package, the overall production-cost structure faced by firms tends to be higher.

Let a firm face a production function such as

$$Q = Q\ (F_1, \ldots, F_r) \qquad (4.38)$$

where $Q$ is the number of units of output produced per time period; and $F_b$ is the number of units employed of input $b$; $b = 1, \ldots, r$.

The cost function faced by the firm is of the following general form:

$$L = L\ (P_1, \ldots, P_r, \ldots) \qquad (4.39)$$

where $L$ is total production costs; and $P_b$ is the total unit price of input $b$; $b = 1, \ldots, r$.

Let the number of units employed of labor be $F_1$; accordingly, the total unit price of labor is given as $P_1$.[26] In the absence of unionization, we let

$$P_1 = P_1' \qquad (4.40)$$

Given $P_1 = P_1'$, the firm's initial total-cost curve is represented in figure 4–7 by the curve $TC'$. If a labor union appears, it presumably will agitate for and eventually attain a higher total unit price of labor. The new value of $P_1$ may then be represented by

$$P_1 = P_1' + \Delta P_1' \qquad (4.41)$$

where $\Delta P_1'$ is the change in the total unit price of labor that results from the labor union's activities.

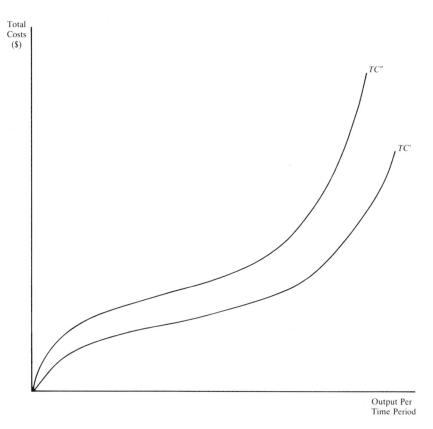

**Figure 4–7.** Effects of Unionization

The new labor price represented in equation 4.41 results in a new and higher total production-cost curve such as $TC''$ in figure 4–7.[27]

The higher cost curves will very likely affect all (or at least most) firms whose employees become unionized. Moreover, the more widespread and the stronger the unions, the more the cost curves can be expected to shift upward. In firms without unions, a similar kind of upshifting of cost curves may well result from various forms of spillovers. As figures 4–5 and 4–6 illustrate, rising cost curves tend to lead to higher product prices (per unit) in both competitive and monopolistic product markets. As the extent of labor unionization increases, the overall level of output prices (living costs) should theoretically rise. This is represented in figure 4–8, where the percentage of the labor force that is unionized is plotted along the abscissa and the cost of living is plotted along the ordinate axis.

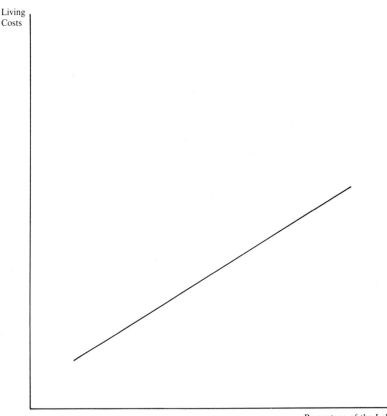

**Figure 4–8.** Living Costs and Unionization

*Empirical Analysis*

The basic model developed in chapters 2 and 3 may now be modified to become the following:

$$Ci = Ci\,(Pi,\ Di,\ Ii,\ Ui) \qquad (4.42)$$

where *Ci, Pi, Di,* and *Ii* are the same as in equation 4.1; and *Ui* is the unionization rate in SMSA *i* expressed as the percentage of the civilian labor force in SMSA *i* that is unionized.

On the basis of equation 4.42, the regression equation to be estimated is of the following form:

$$Cit = e_0t + e_1tPit + e_2tDit + e_3tIit + e_4tUit + \mu t \qquad (4.43)$$

where

$Cit$ is the average annual cost of living in SMSA $i$ during year $t$, for a four-person family living on an intermediate budget;

$e_0t$ is a constant term for year $t$;

$Pit$ is the total population in SMSA $i$ during year $t$;

$Dit$ is the population density in SMSA $i$ for year $t$, expressed in terms of the number of persons per square mile;

$Iit$ is the per-capita income level in SMSA $i$ during year $t$;

$Uit$ is the unionization rate in SMSA $i$ during year $t$;[28] and

$\mu t$ is a stochastic-error term for year $t$.

Equation 4.43 is to be estimated for two years: 1970 and 1978. In both years, there were sufficient data for the analysis of thirty-six SMSAs. These two years were chosen arbitrarily; however, the results obtained for these two cases were essentially identical to the results obtained for all of the other years from 1966 through 1979.

The expected signs of the linear coefficients in equation 4.43 are as follows:

$$e_1t < 0, \ e_2t > 0, \ e_3t > 0, \ \text{and} \ e_4t > 0; \ \text{for all} \ t \qquad (4.44)$$

where $t = 1970$ and 1978.

The ordinary least-squares estimate of equation 4.43 for the year 1970 is given by

$$Ci = +5373.99 - 0.00017Pi + 0.40414Di$$
$$(+5.32) \qquad (-1.89) \qquad (+1.89)$$

$$+ 1.24134Ii + 1.10894Ui$$
$$(+4.32) \qquad (+0.95)$$

$$R^2 = 0.59 \qquad \langle R \rangle_{av}^2 = 0.54 \qquad n = 36 \qquad DF = 31$$

$$F = 11.0868 \qquad \langle C \rangle_{av}i = 10632.62 \qquad (4.45)$$

where terms in parentheses are $t$-values.

The ordinary least-squares estimate of equation 4.43 for the year 1970 is given by

$$Ci = +5373.99 - 0.00017Pi + 0.40414Di$$
$$\quad\ (+5.32) \qquad (-1.89) \qquad\ (+1.89)$$

$$+ 1.24134Ii + 1.10894Ui$$
$$\quad (+4.32) \qquad (+0.95)$$

$$R^2 = 0.59 \qquad \langle R \rangle_{av}{}^2 = 0.54 \qquad n = 36 \qquad DF = 31$$

$$F = 11.0868 \qquad \langle C \rangle_{av}i = 10632.62 \tag{4.45}$$

where terms in parentheses are $t$-values.

All four of the estimated coefficients in equation 4.45 have the expected signs. The coefficient of the income variable is statistically significant at beyond the 0.01 level, whereas the coefficients of the population-size and population-density variables are statistically significant at approximately the 0.06 level. The coefficient of the unionization rate variable is not statistically significant at even the 0.15 level. The $R^2$ value is 0.59 and the $\langle R \rangle_{av}{}^2$ is 0.54, so that the model explains nearly three-fifths of the variation in the living-cost variable. The $F$-ratio is statistically significant at the 0.01 level.

There are four cases of multicollinearity among the variables in equation 4.45:

1. $Pi$ and $Di$, at $+0.89$;
2. $Pi$ and $Ii$, at $+0.63$;
3. $Di$ and $Ii$, at $+0.59$; and
4. $Ui$ and $Ii$, at $+0.51$.

These instances of multicollinearity account for at least some of the weakness of the coefficients for the variables $Pi$, $Di$, and $Ui$. Multicollinearity notwithstanding, the weakness of the unionization-rate variable cannot be fundamentally attributed to its correlation of $+0.51$ with per-capita income.

The ordinary least-squares estimate of equation 4.43 for the year 1978 is

$$Ci = +13116.20 - 0.00012Pi + 0.61656Di$$
$$\quad\ (+3.30) \qquad\ (-0.39) \qquad\ (+1.16)$$

$$+ 0.51294Ii + 4.07715Ui$$
$$\quad (+0.92) \qquad (+0.95)$$

$$R^2 = 0.20 \qquad \langle R \rangle_{av}{}^2 = 0.10 \qquad n = 36 \qquad DF = 31$$

$$F = 1.92138 \qquad \langle C \rangle_{av} i = 18261.21 \tag{4.46}$$

where terms in parentheses are $t$-values.

Although all four estimated coefficients exhibit the hypothesized signs, none is statistically significant at an acceptable level in equation 4.46. As one would logically expect, the $R^2$, $\langle R \rangle_{av}{}^2$, and $F$-ratios are all extremely low in this regression estimate.

In neither equation 4.45 nor equation 4.46 does the unionization-rate variable exhibit a satisfactory level of statistical significance. This same empirical finding is obtained when estimating equation 4.43 for the other years from 1966 through 1979.

In an effort to gain further insight into the possible impact of the unionization-rate variable on living costs, three more regressions (4.47, 4.48, and 4.49) involving $Ui$ are to be estimated.

$$Ci = f_0 + f_1 Pi + f_2 Di + f_3 Ii + f_4 Ui + f_5 Ti + f \tag{4.47}$$

$$Ci = g_0 + g_1 Pi + g_2 Di + g_3 Ii + g_4 Ui + g_5 Ti + g_6 Ri + g \tag{4.48}$$

$$Ci = h_0 + h_1 Pi + h_2 Di + h_3 Ii + h_4 Ui + h_5 Ri + h \tag{4.49}$$

where

$Ci$, $Pi$, $Di$, $Ii$, $Ui$, $Ti$, and $Ri$ are as before;

$f_0$, $g_0$, and $h_0$ are constant terms; and $f$, $g$, and $h$ are stochastic-error terms.

All three equations are to be estimated for the years 1970 and 1978.

The ordinary least-squares estimate of regression equation 4.47 for the year 1970 is

$$Ci = +5699.24 - 0.00020Pi + 0.45691Di$$
$$(+5.74) \qquad (-2.26) \qquad (+2.19)$$

$$+ 1.02574Ii + 1.06268Ui + 2.54424Ti$$
$$(+3.38) \qquad (+0.94) \qquad (+1.77)$$

$$R^2 = 0.63 \qquad \langle R \rangle_{av}{}^2 = 0.57 \qquad n = 36 \qquad DF = 30$$

$$F = 10.1142 \qquad \langle C \rangle_{av}i = 10632.62 \qquad\qquad (4.50)$$

where terms in parentheses are $t$-values.

The ordinary least-squares estimate of equation 4.48 for the year 1970 is given by

$$Ci = +7033.27 - 0.00015Pi + 0.38100Di + 0.96853Ii$$
$$\quad (+6.52) \qquad (-1.79) \qquad (+1.94) \qquad (+3.42)$$

$$- 1.48716Ui + 1.38781Ti - 797.809Ri$$
$$\quad (-0.99) \qquad (+0.98) \qquad (-2.39)$$

$$R^2 = 0.69 \qquad \langle R \rangle_{av}^2 = 0.62 \qquad n = 36 \qquad DF = 29$$

$$F = 10.6973 \qquad \langle C \rangle_{av}i = 10632.62 \qquad\qquad (4.51)$$

where terms in parentheses are $t$-values.

The ordinary least-squares estimate of equation 4.49 for the year 1970 is the following:

$$Ci = +7063.35 - 0.00013Pi + 0.34494Di$$
$$\quad (+6.55) \qquad (-1.59) \qquad (+1.79)$$

$$+ 1.06440Ii - 1.82191Ui - 909.521Ri$$
$$\quad (+4.01) \qquad (-1.25) \qquad (-2.90)$$

$$R^2 = 0.68 \qquad \langle R \rangle_{av}^2 = 0.62 \qquad n = 36 \qquad DF = 30$$

$$F = 12.6634 \qquad \langle C \rangle_{av}i = 10632.62 \qquad\qquad (4.52)$$

where terms in parentheses are $t$-values.

The ordinary least-squares estimate of equation 4.47 for the year 1978 is given by

$$Ci = +13116.50 - 0.00013Pi + 0.61486Di$$
$$\quad (+3.25) \qquad (-0.39) \qquad (+1.13)$$

$$+ 0.50617Ii + 4.10376Ui + 0.17593Ti$$
$$\quad (+0.87) \qquad (+0.93) \qquad (+0.05)$$

$$R^2 = 0.20 \qquad \langle R \rangle_{av}^2 = 0.07 \qquad n = 36 \qquad DF = 30$$

$$F = 1.48810 \qquad \langle C \rangle_{av} i = 18261.21 \tag{4.53}$$

where terms in parentheses are $t$-values.

The ordinary least-squares estimate of equation 4.48 for the year 1978 is given by

$$Ci = +15238.41 - 0.00008Pi + 0.65642Di + 0.41808Ii$$
$$\phantom{Ci = }(+3.17) \qquad (-0.26) \qquad (+1.20) \qquad (+0.70)$$

$$- 0.09017Ui - 0.84279Ti - 1111.15Ri$$
$$(-0.01) \qquad (-0.22) \qquad (-0.82)$$

$$R^2 = 0.22 \qquad \langle R \rangle_{av}^2 = 0.05 \qquad n = 36 \qquad DF = 29$$

$$F = 1.33885 \qquad \langle C \rangle_{av} i = 18261.21 \tag{4.54}$$

where terms in parentheses are $t$-values.

Estimating equation 4.49 by ordinary least-squares for the year 1978 yields

$$Ci = +15061.14 - 0.00010Pi + 0.64559Di$$
$$\phantom{Ci = }(+3.23) \qquad (-0.33) \qquad (+1.20)$$

$$+ 0.39635Ii + 0.37709Ui - 1017.69Ri$$
$$(+0.69) \qquad (+0.06) \qquad (-0.81)$$

$$R^2 = 0.22 \qquad \langle R \rangle_{av}^2 = 0.08 \qquad n = 36 \qquad DF = 30$$

$$F = 1.64966 \qquad \langle C \rangle_{av} i = 18261.21 \tag{4.55}$$

where terms in parentheses are $t$-values.

In equations 4.50 through 4.55, the unionization rate is examined in the context of three different specifications for two different years, 1970 and 1978. In all six cases, the coefficient of the variable $Ui$ fails to be statistically significant at even the 0.10 level. It could be inferred that the variable $Ui$ does not satisfactorily replace the variable $Ri$ in terms of explanatory power. The same conclusion is reached when regression equations 4.47 through

4.49 are estimated for other years in the time span from 1966 through 1979.[29]

## More on Right-to-Work Laws

As evidenced in the works by Burtt (1979), Ehrenberg and Smith (1982), Peterson (1963), and Reynolds (1982), the issue of the effects of right-to-work laws has long been the subject of much controversy and concern. The treatment in this book of right-to-work legislation and its potential effects has been unique. This uniqueness derives from the fact that right-to-work legislation is viewed here as having significant economic effects not only on labor-market structures per se but also on the overall structure of final commodity prices in the marketplace.

Since nearly every regression estimate presented here thus far has found that right-to-work legislation profoundly influences geographic living-cost levels and geographic living-cost differentials, a more in-depth empirical analysis of the relationship between right-to-work laws and living costs is called for.

In order to gain further insights into the hypothesized cause-and-effect relationship between right-to-work laws and living-cost levels, the following three models will be considered:

$$Ci = Ci\ (Ri) \tag{4.56}$$

$$Ci = Ci\ (Ri,\ Pi) \tag{4.57}$$

$$Ci = Ci\ (Ri,\ Pi,\ Di) \tag{4.58}$$

where

$Ci$ is a measure of the cost of living in SMSA $i$;

$Ri$ is an indicator of the presence of right-to-work legislation in SMSA $i$;

$Di$ is the population density in SMSA $i$; and

$Pi$ is the total population of SMSA $i$.

The following restrictions on the partial derivatives are imposed:

$$\partial Ci/\partial Ri < 0 \tag{4.59}$$

$$\partial Ci/\partial Pi < 0 \tag{4.60}$$

$$\partial Ci/\partial Di > 0. \tag{4.61}$$

The relationship represented in equation 4.59, of course, posits the basic relationship between right-to-work laws and living costs.

The actual linear regression equations to be estimated are as follows:[30]

$$Ci = j_0 + j_1 Ri + j \tag{4.62}$$

$$Ci = k_0 + k_1 Ri + k_2 Pi + k \tag{4.63}$$

$$Ci = l_0 + l_1 Ri + l_2 Pi + l_3 Di + l \tag{4.64}$$

where

$Ci, Ri, Pi,$ and $Di$ are as earlier indicated;

$j_0, k_0,$ and $l_0$ are constant terms; and

$j, k,$ and $l,$ are stochastic-error terms.

On the basis of equation 4.59, we should expect that

$$j_1, k_1, l_1 < 0. \tag{4.65}$$

From equation 4.60, it follows that we should expect that

$$k_2, l_2 < 0. \tag{4.66}$$

Finally, equation 4.61 implies that

$$l_3 > 0. \tag{4.67}$$

Equations 4.62 through 4.64 are to be estimated for three years: 1970, 1972, and 1979.[31] These three years were chosen entirely at random. For the year 1970, thirty-nine SMSAs were available for study. For the year 1972, thirty-six SMSAs were studied; data availability considerations precluded an analysis of three SMSAs during 1972. For the year 1979, sufficient data were available for the analysis of only twenty-four SMSAs.

Estimating regression equations 4.62 through 4.64 for the year 1970 yields equations 4.68 through 4.70:

$$Ci = +10893.53 - 1079.83Ri$$
$$(+93.6) \qquad (-4.46)$$

$$R^2 = 0.35 \qquad \langle R \rangle_{av}{}^2 = 0.33 \qquad n = 39 \qquad DF = 37$$

$$F = 19.8591 \qquad \langle C \rangle_{av} i = 10644.32 \tag{4.68}$$

$$Ci = +10704.60 - 955.126Ri + 0.00008Pi$$
$$\phantom{Ci = }(+70.2) \qquad (-3.91) \qquad (+1.84)$$

$$R^2 = 0.41 \qquad \langle R \rangle_{av}{}^2 = 0.37 \qquad n = 39 \qquad DF = 36$$

$$F = 12.2597 \qquad \langle C \rangle_{av} i = 10644.32 \tag{4.69}$$

$$Ci = +10535.40 - 837.295Ri$$
$$\phantom{Ci = }(+77.4) \qquad (-4.01)$$

$$\phantom{Ci = } - 0.00017Pi + 0.70704Di$$
$$\phantom{Ci = xx}(-2.23) \qquad (+3.91)$$

$$R^2 = 0.59 \qquad \langle R \rangle_{av}{}^2 = 0.55 \qquad n = 39 \qquad DF = 35$$

$$F = 16.5086 \qquad \langle C \rangle_{av} i = 10644.32 \tag{4.70}$$

where terms in parentheses are $t$-values.

In equation 4.68, the right-to-work-law variable $(Ri)$ has the expected negative sign and is statistically significant at beyond the 0.01 level. In equation 4.69, the right-to-work-law variable again has the expected negative sign and is statistically significant at beyond the 0.01 level. Note, however, that the population-size variable $(Pi)$ has the wrong sign and an insignificant coefficient.[32] In equation 4.70, the right-to-work-law coefficient exhibits the expected negative sign; it is also statistically significant at well beyond the 0.01 level. The population-size coefficient exhibits the hypothesized sign and a coefficient that is statistically significant at well beyond the 0.05 level. The population-density variable $(Di)$ is statistically significant at well beyond the 0.01 level with the expected sign. Contrasting the results in equations 4.69 and 4.70 implies the possibility that the variable $Di$ may be classified as an "omitted variable."[33]

Estimating equations 4.62 through 4.64 for the year 1972 yields equations 4.71 through 4.73:

$$Ci = +11634.01 - 1292.82Ri$$
$$\phantom{Ci = }(+86.8) \qquad (-4.25)$$

$$R^2 = 0.35 \qquad \langle R \rangle_{av}{}^2 = 0.33 \qquad n = 36 \qquad DF = 34$$

$$F = 18.0792 \qquad \langle C \rangle_{av} i = 11382.62 \tag{4.71}$$

$$Ci = +11371.64 - 1164.91Ri + 0.00012Pi$$
$$\phantom{Ci = }(+65.7) \qquad (-3.97) \qquad (+2.23)$$

$$R^2 = 0.43 \qquad \langle R \rangle_{av}^2 = 0.40 \qquad n = 36 \qquad DF = 33$$

$$F = 12.5834 \qquad \langle C \rangle_{av} i = 11382.62 \tag{4.72}$$

$$Ci = +11129.80 - 984.679Ri$$
$$\phantom{Ci = }(+76.4) \qquad (-4.21)$$

$$\phantom{Ci = }- 0.00015Pi + 0.78872Di$$
$$\phantom{Ci = -}(-2.08) \qquad (+4.63)$$

$$R^2 = 0.66 \qquad \langle R \rangle_{av}^2 = 0.63 \qquad n = 36 \qquad DF = 32$$

$$F = 20.7315 \qquad \langle C \rangle_{av} i = 11382.62 \tag{4.73}$$

where terms in parentheses below coefficients are signed $t$-values.

In equation 4.71, the coefficient of the right-to-work-law variable is statistically significant with the expected negative sign at far beyond the 0.01 level. In equation 4.72, the coefficient of the right-to-work-law variable is negative and statistically significant at beyond the 0.01 level. In equation 4.72, however, the coefficient of the population-size variable has a positive sign; in addition, this coefficient is statistically significant at beyond the 0.05 level. Clearly, this runs entirely counter to the ceteris paribus expectations in 4.66. Finally, in equation 4.73, the estimated coefficients of all three exogenous variables have the correct signs. In addition, two of the estimated coefficients are statistically significant at well beyond the 0.01 level, and the third estimated coefficient is statistically significant at the 0.05 level. Contrasting regressions 4.72 and 4.73 reveals that, as was the case for the year 1970, the addition of the population-density variable alters the sign on the variable for population size. Thus, there once again appears to be substantive evidence that the variable $Di$ is an omitted variable. If this is in fact the case, then there is omitted-variable bias in regression estimate 4.72.[34] A similar bias may also exist in equation 4.69.

The ordinary least-squares estimate of equations 4.62 through 4.64 for the year 1979 yields equations 4.74 through 4.76:

$$Ci = +21381.50 - 2440.25Ri$$
$$\phantom{Ci = }(+63.8) \qquad (-2.97)$$

$$R^2 = 0.29 \qquad \langle R \rangle_{av}{}^2 = 0.25 \qquad n = 24 \qquad DF = 22$$

$$F = 8.83223 \qquad \langle C \rangle_{av}i = 20974.83 \tag{4.74}$$

$$Ci = \underset{(+36.1)}{+21212.82} - \underset{(-2.80)}{2385.35Ri} + \underset{(+0.35)}{0.00005Pi}$$

$$R^2 = 0.29 \qquad \langle R \rangle_{av}{}^2 = 0.22 \qquad n = 24 \qquad DF = 21$$

$$F = 4.30262 \qquad \langle C \rangle_{av}i = 20974.23 \tag{4.75}$$

$$Ci = \underset{(+42.5)}{+21417.91} - \underset{(-2.67)}{1963.17Ri}$$

$$- \underset{(-2.08)}{0.00004Pi} + \underset{(+3.03)}{1.03733Di}$$

$$R^2 = 0.51 \qquad \langle R \rangle_{av}{}^2 = 0.44 \qquad n = 24 \qquad DF = 20$$

$$F = 7.04800 \qquad \langle C \rangle_{av}i = 20974.23 \tag{4.76}$$

where terms in parentheses are $t$-values.

The pattern of results for the year 1979 is remarkably similar to the patterns for 1970 and 1972. In equation 4.74, the coefficient of the right-to-work-law variable ($Ri$) exhibits the hypothesized negative sign and is statistically significant at beyond the 0.01 level. In equation 4.75, the coefficient of the right-to-work-law variable is again statistically significant at the 0.01 level with the correct sign. The coefficient of the variable for population-size ($Pi$), however, exhibits the wrong sign and fails to be statistically significant at even the 0.20 level. In equation 4.76, the coefficients of all three independent variables have the correct signs. The coefficients of the variables $Ri$ and $Di$ are statistically significant at the 0.01 level, whereas the coefficient of the variable $Pi$ is statistically significant at 0.05 level. As was the case for the years 1970 and 1972, contrasting equations 4.75 and 4.76 reveals evidence of omitted-variable bias with respect to the variable $Di$.

Equations 4.68 through 4.76 all indicate that the right-to-work-law variable is a strong and consistent explanatory variable. This same basic finding was obtained for all of the other years from 1966 through 1979. It may be concluded that right-to-work legislation acts strongly and consistently to generate lower living costs.

The results of equations 4.68 through 4.76 notwithstanding, there are apparently several instances of possible omitted-variable bias in the specified systems. In an effort to gain a potentially different perspective on the living-cost/right-to-work-law issue, a different set of estimations will be undertaken. This set of estimations consists of regression equations 4.62, 4.64, and the following regression:[35]

$$Ci = q_0 + q_1 Ri + q_2 Di + q \tag{4.77}$$

where

    $Ci$, $Ri$, and $Di$ are as in equation 4.1;

    $q_0$ is a constant term; and

    $q$ is a stochastic-error term.

The equations 4.62, 4.77, and 4.64 are to be estimated for the single year 1976. Estimating the three regressions in question for 1976 yields:[36]

$$Ci = +16546.00 - 1588.11 Ri$$
$$\phantom{Ci = }(+88.2) \phantom{xxxxx} (-3.71)$$

$$R^2 = 0.30 \phantom{xx} \langle R \rangle_{av}^2 = 0.24 \phantom{xx} n = 38 \phantom{xx} DF = 36$$

$$F = 15.29957 \phantom{xx} \langle C \rangle_{av} i = 16143.14 \tag{4.78}$$

$$Ci = +16069.06 - 1246.88 Ri + 0.49307 Di$$
$$\phantom{Ci = }(+71.6) \phantom{xxxx} (-4.24) \phantom{xxxx} (+3.47)$$

$$R^2 = 0.48 \phantom{xx} \langle R \rangle_{av}^2 = 0.40 \phantom{xx} n = 38 \phantom{xx} DF = 35$$

$$F = 16.09271 \phantom{xx} \langle C \rangle_{av} i = 16143.14 \tag{4.79}$$

$$Ci = +16194.92 - 1260.28 Ri$$
$$\phantom{Ci = }(+39.6) \phantom{xxxx} (-4.33)$$

$$\phantom{Ci = } + 0.73489 Di - 0.00016 Pi$$
$$\phantom{Ci = xx}(+3.28) \phantom{xxxx} (-1.20)$$

$$R^2 = 0.50 \phantom{xx} \langle R \rangle_{av}^2 = 0.41 \phantom{xx} n = 38 \phantom{xx} DF = 34$$

$$F = 11.44575 \phantom{xx} \langle C \rangle_{av} i = 16143.14 \tag{4.80}$$

where terms in parentheses are $t$-values.

In equation 4.78, the estimated coefficient of the right-to-work-law variable is negative (as expected) and statistically significant at the 0.01 level. In equation 4.79, the estimated coefficients of both exogenous variables are statistically significant at the 0.01 level with the expected signs. In equation 4.80, two out of the three estimated coefficients are statistically significant at the 0.01 level with the expected signs; only the population-size variable is not statistically significant at an acceptable level.[37] Thus, we may once again conclude that right-to-work legislation acts to generate a lower overall level of the cost of living in an area. The strength of this conclusion is increased by observing the persistently high values for the coefficient of determination that result from the variable $Ri$ by itself.[38]

**Summary and Conclusions**

This chapter has attempted to extend the basic model developed in chapters 2 and 3. The extensions developed included:

1.  the examination of a variable to allow for geographic utility-price differentials;
2.  the examination of the potential effects of property taxation on living costs;
3.  the consideration of an alternative variable to $Ri$ to reflect labor-market structures and conditions; and
4.  the consideration of a more in-depth empirical analysis of the effects of right-to-work laws on living costs.

The addition of the utility-price variable did not measurably improve the strength of the basic model. The utility-price variable itself did achieve a reasonably high degree of statistical significance in the regression estimates for the years 1971, 1973, 1974, and 1975. For the most part, however, the inclusion of the utility-price variable was associated with lower $t$-values of the coefficients for the variables $Pi$, $Di$, $Ii$, and $Ri$ in the basic model.

The property-tax variable was measured by the per-capita property-tax level in each SMSA. In the regression estimates examined in this chapter, the coefficient of the property-tax variable was very consistently insignificant. The property-tax level did not on the whole explain geographic living-cost levels.[39] In point of fact, the principal statistical impact of adding geographic property-tax differentials to the model was to diminish, often quite sharply, the $t$-values of and the statistical significance levels of the coefficients for the variables $Pi$, $Di$, $Ii$, and $Ri$. In general, the basic model from chapter 3 provided far stronger regression results when the property-tax variable was omitted entirely.

Similarly, the substitution of a unionization-rate variable for the right-to-work-law dummy variable (0, 1) acted principally to lower the statistical significance levels of the coefficients for the variables $Pi$, $Di$, $Ii$, and $Ri$. In no instance did the unionization-rate variable act to measurably improve the explanatory power of the model. Overall, the unionization-rate variable was inferior to the right-to-work-law variable in terms of the ability to generate statistically significant empirical results.

Finally, the in-depth empirical analysis of the right-to-work-law variable yielded twelve new regression estimates. In all twelve cases, the coefficient of this variable performed very well; generally, the coefficient of the variable $Ri$ was statistically significant at the 0.01 level or beyond. The analysis in this chapter succeeded in further quantifying and emphasizing the extraordinary power of right-to-work legislation in explaining living-cost levels in and living-cost differentials among SMSAs in the United States.

On the basis of the findings in this chapter and the previous chapter, the following conclusions regarding the variables in the basic model have largely been reinforced:

$$\partial Ci/\partial Ri < 0 \qquad (4.81)$$

$$\partial Ci/\partial Pi < 0 \qquad (4.82)$$

$$\partial Ci/\partial Di > 0 \qquad (4.83)$$

$$\partial Ci/\partial Ii > 0. \qquad (4.84)$$

The economic and public-policy implications of these findings will be explored in chapter 6.

## Notes

1. It is essential to bear in mind that when utility prices are said to *directly* influence living costs, it is because the utilities are themselves being directly consumed by households.

2. Related to price-elasticity, see, for example, Bilas (1967), Baumol (1965), or Ferguson (1972).

3. Of course, if the unit price of *unused* utilities should rise, there would be no direct change in the costs for the firm in question. However, if the utility price should rise and affect the cost structure of firms supplying inputs to the firm in question, its cost schedules would still shift upward.

4. Of course, when economic profits are zero, the firm still is earning normal profits.

5. This observation also obtains for the competitive case.

6. The literal interpretation of $Ai$ is "cents per 10 therms in SMSA $i$." One therm contains approximately 100 cubic feet of natural gas.

7. Data on variable $Ai$ are unavailable by SMSA for the year 1966.

8. Actually, the coefficient of the variable $Ai$ in equation 4.17 is not even statistically significant at the 0.10 level.

9. In this chapter, the explanatory power of the model is higher for the year 1970 than for any of the previously-examined years.

10. The equation in question is regression estimate 4.18.

11. The minimum acceptable significance level is 0.05.

12. Both cases of multcollinearity do, nonetheless, contribute to a somewhat weakened performance by the population-density variable in equation 4.22.

13. In point of fact, neither of these two variables is statistically significant at even the 0.15 level in equation 4.23.

14. Related to the effects of OPEC pricing policies, see Cebula and Frewer (1980).

15. This testing involves three different years.

16. It is not essential to distinguish here among the various forms of public goods. It is also unnecessary to specify whether $m \gtrless n$. In fact, it is even possible that $m = n$. Such an issue, though of potential interest, is not relevant to the present analysis.

17. As defined here, $P_a$ is *net* of all direct taxes on $a; a = 1, \ldots, n$.

18. Related to the treatment of property taxation in the Internal Revenue Code, see Aaron (1970).

19. These institutional considerations might, among other things, include rent-control regulations.

20. The relationship shown in equation 4.26 derives from the following function: $C = C (P_1, \ldots, P_n, TPr, T\text{-}TPr)$.

21. Of course, the firm can escape taxation of this sort if it succeeds in attaining tax-exempt status. Naturally, one would not expect such a status to be sustained indefinitely.

22. For a classic exposition of tax shifting, see Musgrave (1958).

23. There are alternatives to using the *per-capita* property-tax level. Nevertheless, since this study is oriented toward the average level of living costs, a per-capita specification seems appropriate and entirely defensible.

24. For the years 1974 and 1975, the property-tax data are from the year 1972.

25. For the year 1978, the property tax data are from the year 1977.

26. Since $P_1$ is the *total* unit price of labor, it obviously includes both the wage rate and the value of fringe benefits (prorated).

27. The cost curves *may* not shift if there are inputs in the firm's production function that can perfectly substitute for labor. Perfect substi-

tutes were originally discussed by Hicks (1946); see also the paper by Cebula (1972).

28. There are no data that directly yield the percentage of the civilian labor force that is unionized in each SMSA. The procedure adopted for computing *Uit* here is similar in principle to that used earlier to determine the value of *Rit*. *Uit* was approximated (admittedly rather crudely) by using the percentage of the civilian labor force in the state in which SMSA *i* was principally located.

29. In fact, the same basic results were obtained for *all* of the years in question. In addition, the pattern of nearly general statistical insignificance of other coefficients, as exhibited in equations 4.50 through 4.55, is found in *all* of the other estimations.

30. To avoid notational difficulties, the symbol *i* was not used as a coefficient in the regression equations.

31. The same essential results as those obtained for 1970, 1972, and 1979 have been obtained as well for the other years from 1966 through 1979.

32. That is to say, the coefficient on variable *Pi* fails to be statistically significant at the 0.05 level.

33. Related to the concept of the omitted variable, see the recent studies by Renas and Kumar (1978 and 1981).

34. A similar problem has been found in Cebula (1979).

35. Equation 4.77 replaces equation 4.63. This fact accounts for the equation sequence 4.62–4.77–4.64.

36. The year 1976 was chosen at random. Nevertheless, the results in equations 4.78 through 4.80 are essentially the same for all of the years in the period under study.

37. The coefficient of the variable *Pi,* however, is negative (as expected).

38. See equations 4.68, 4.71, 4.74, and 4.78.

39. This conforms to the general arguments in Herber (1971, p. 233).

## References

Aaron, H. 1970. "Income Taxes and Housing." *American Economic Review* 60:789–806.

Baumol, W. 1965. *Economic Theory and Operations Analysis*. Englewood Cliffs, N.J.: Prentice-Hall.

Bilas, R. 1967. *Microeconomic Theory: A Graphical Analysis*. New York: McGraw-Hill.

Burtt, E.J. 1979. *Labor in the American Economy*. New York: St. Martin's Press.

———. 1972. "Perfect Substitutes: Some Notes." *Rivista Internazionale di Scienze Economiche e Commerciali* 19:894–905.

Cebula, R.J. 1979. *The Determinants of Human Migration*. Lexington, Mass.: D.C. Heath, Lexington Books.

Cebula, R.J., and Frewer, M. 1980. "Oil Imports and Inflation: An Empirical International Analysis of the 'Imported' Inflation Thesis." *Kyklos* 33:4, 615–622.

Ehrenberg, R.G., and Smith, R.S. 1982. *Modern Labor Economics: Theory and Public Policy*. Glenview, Ill.: Scott, Foresman.

Ferguson, C.E. 1972. *Microeconomic Theory*. Homewood, Ill.: Irwin.

Herber, B.P. 1971. *Modern Public Finance*. Homewood, Ill.: Irwin.

Hicks, J.R. 1946. *Value and Capital*. Oxford, England: Clarendon Press.

Maxwell, J.A. 1969. *Financing State and Local Governments*. Washington, D.C.: Brookings Institution.

Musgrave, R. 1958. *The Theory of Public Finance*. New York: Macmillan.

Netzer, D. 1966. *Economics of the Property Tax*. Washington, D.C.: Brookings Institution.

Peterson, F. 1963. *American Labor Unions*. New York: Harper and Row.

Renas, S.M., and Kumar, R. 1978. "The Cost of Living, Labor Market Opportunities, and the Migration Decision: A Case of Misspecification?" *Annals of Regional Science* 12:95–104.

———. 1981. "The Cost of Living, Labor Market Opportunities, and the Migration Decision: Some Additional Evidence." *Annals of Regional Science* 15:74–79.

Reynolds, L.G. 1982. *Labor Economics and Labor Relations*. Englewood Cliffs, N.J.: Prentice-Hall.

# 5

# A Simple Dynamic Analysis: Geographic Inflation-Rate Differentials in the United States

The emphasis in the first four chapters of this book has been on living-cost *levels*. By focusing exclusively on levels of living costs and of living-cost differentials, the analysis has restricted itself to a rather *static* frame of reference. The present chapter seeks to go beyond the implicit limitations of strictly static analysis by attempting to develop a more dynamic model. This dynamic model will focus on geographic (regional) inflation-rate differentials. The *regional inflation rate* is here defined as the rate of change of the living-cost level in a region.

Before developing a model to explain inflation-rate differentials among regions, the potential economic importance of such differentials should be discussed. A model will then be theoretically developed and empirically analyzed.

## The Potential Importance of Geographic Inflation-Rate Differentials

As observed in chapter 1, several studies have examined the impact on migration of geographic living-cost differentials.[1] A study by Renas and Kumar (1978) considers not only the impact of living-cost levels but also the impact of inflation-rate levels on migration. The basic model examined by Renas and Kumar (1978) is given by

$$Mi = F(Yi, Ci, YCHi, CCHi, Ui, Ei, DDi, Di) \qquad (5.1)$$

where

$Mi$ is the net number of migrants into SMSA $i$ between 1960 and 1970 expressed as a percentage of the 1960 population;

$Yi$ is the median family income in SMSA $i$ in 1969;

$Ci$ is the annual cost in SMSA $i$ of an intermediate budget for a four-person family in spring, 1969;

$YCHi$ is the annual rate of change of median family income in SMSA $i$ between 1959 and 1969, expressed as a percentage; and

*CCHi* is the annual rate of change in the cost of living in SMSA *i*, expressed as a percentage, based on the change in the annual cost of an intermediate budget for a four-person family between spring, 1967, and spring, 1970. This variable is the regional inflation rate.

*Ui* is the unemployment rate of the civilian labor force in SMSA *i* in 1960;

*Ei* is the median school years completed in 1960 for the population twenty-five years old and over in SMSA *i;*

*DDi* is annual degree days, 65° base in SMSA *i;* and

*Di* is population per square mile in 1960 in SMSA *i*.

Renas and Kumar (1978) argue that the following relationships should be expected:

$$\partial F/\partial Yi > 0,\ \partial F/\partial Ci < 0,\ \partial F/\partial YCHi > 0,\ \partial F/\partial CCHi < 0,\ \partial F/\partial Ui < 0,$$

$$\partial F/\partial DDi < 0,\ \text{and}\ \partial F/\partial Di < 0. \tag{5.2}$$

In addition, they argue that

$$\partial F/\partial Ei \gtreqless 0. \tag{5.3}$$

Thus, for the variable *Ei*, Renas and Kumar (1978) must apply a two-pronged test.

Renas and Kumar (1978) proceed to estimate the following three forms of regression equation (by ordinary least squares):

$$Mi = a_0 + a_1 Yi + a_2 YCHi + a_3 Ui + a_4 Ei + a_5 DDi + a_6 Di + a_7 \tag{5.4}$$

$$Mi = b_0 + b_1 Yi + b_2 Ci + b_3 YCHi + b_4 CCHi + b_5 Ui + b_6 Ei + b_7 DDi$$

$$+ b_8 Di + b_9 \tag{5.5}$$

$$Mi = c_0 + c_1 Yi + c_2 Ci + c_3 YCHi + c_4 Ui + c_5 Ei + c_6 DDi + c_7 \tag{5.6}$$

where

*Mi, Yi, YCHi, Ci, CCHi, Ui, Ei, DDi,* and *Di* are as in equation 5.1;

$a_0$, $b_0$, and $c_0$ are constant terms; and

$a_7$, $b_9$, and $c_7$ are stochastic-error terms.

The empirical findings by Renas and Kumar (1978) are not entirely conclusive. Nevertheless, they do find that migrants are not subject to money illusion. Accordingly, factors such as regional living-cost levels and regional inflation rates—through their influence over time on living standards—are logically factors in migrants' long-run decisions.

If future research should find that differential inflation rates do in fact significantly affect geographic mobility, then it will also be true that such inflation rates influence regional labor markets and geographic resource allocation. Differential inflation rates may well act to influence the political and economic environment in very important ways.

## The Dynamic Model: Determinants of Regional Inflation Rates

In this analysis, the *regional inflation rate* will measure the *percentage rate of growth of the cost of living in an area*. This statistical definition conforms in principle to the earlier definition given for regional inflation rate. The regional inflation rate is hypothesized here to depend on four basic variables: the net in-migration rate, the percentage rate of growth in the per-capita income level, the percentage rate of growth in the proportion of the civilian labor force that is unionized, and the percentage rate of growth of per-capita state plus local taxation levels.

### Net In-Migration and Regional Inflation Rates

In this section it is hypothesized that regional inflation rates are affected by rates of net in-migration. Presumably, when people migrate to a community, they influence both the total population of that community and the size of the civilian labor force in that community.

The greater the net in-migration rate to an area, the more rapidly that area's total population grows. In turn, a greater total population implies the appearance of *agglomeration economies*. As noted in chapter 2, the ultimate effect of agglomeration economies is a reduction in the costs of production of goods and services. In a dynamic context, than, the greater the net in-migration rate, the greater the rate of reduction in production costs because of agglomeration economies. Naturally, the greater the rate of reduction in production costs, the greater the rate of reduction in the regional inflation rate over time.[2] Hence, the greater the net in-migration rate to an area (region), the lower that area's regional inflation rate. This relationship is depicted graphically in figure 5–1, where the regional inflation rate is plotted vertically and the rate of net in-migration is plotted horizontally.

As net in-migration to a region occurs, the civilian labor force also grows. Of course, the rate of growth in the civilian labor force depends critically on the labor-force participation rate of the in-migrants. The labor-force participation rate in turn depends critically on the age structure of the population. This is illustrated in table 5–1, where the labor-force participation rate of the civilian labor force is listed by age group for selected years. From table 5–1, it can be inferred that the greater the extent to which the net migration rate into an area consists of persons in the 20–64 age category, the greater the extent to which the area's net in-migration rate leads to growth in the area's civilian labor force.

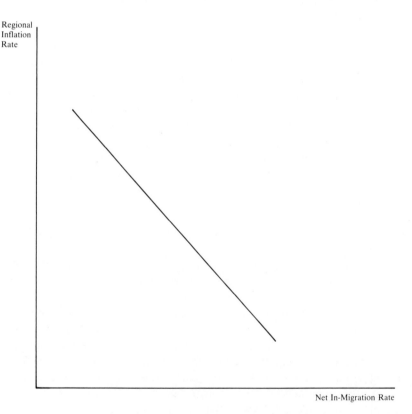

**Figure 5–1.** Effects of Net Migration

**Table 5–1**
**Labor-Force Participation Rate, by Age Group**

| Year and Age Group | Participation (percentage) |
|---|---|
| 1970 | |
| 20–24 | 85.1 |
| 25–34 | 95.0 |
| 35–44 | 95.7 |
| 45–54 | 92.9 |
| 55–64 | 81.5 |
| 65 and over | 25.8 |
| 1975 | |
| 20–24 | 84.6 |
| 25–34 | 94.2 |
| 35–44 | 94.8 |
| 45–54 | 91.1 |
| 55–64 | 74.8 |
| 65 and over | 20.8 |
| 1977 | |
| 20–24 | 85.3 |
| 25–34 | 94.2 |
| 35–44 | 94.9 |
| 45–54 | 90.3 |
| 55–64 | 73.0 |
| 65 and over | 19.3 |

Source: U.S. Bureau of the Census, *Statistical Abstract of the United States, 1978*, Table 644. Washington, D.C., U.S. Government Printing Office, 1978.

The greater the rate of growth of an area's civilian labor force, the slower the growth rate of that area's wage-rate structure. This is shown in part in figure 5–2, where the number of persons in the civilian labor force is plotted along the abscissa and the wage rate is plotted along the ordinate axis. The initial wage rate is shown at point A, which is at the intersection of labor-supply curve SS and labor-demand curve DD. As the size of the area's civilian labor force grows through, say, net in-migration, the labor-supply curve shifts to the right to point S'S' and the money-wage rate falls to that wage-rate value associated with point B. Clearly, the more rapidly the labor supply grows, the further to the right the labor-supply curve shifts and the greater the decline in the money-wage rate. If the labor-demand schedule shifts to the right over time at a faster rate than the labor-supply schedule shifts, money-wage rates will rise; nevertheless, the rise in the money-wage rate is obviously a decreasing function of the rate of increase in the area's supply of labor.

Mathematically, the money-wage rate, $W$, depends upon

$$W = W (Ns, Nd) \tag{5.7}$$

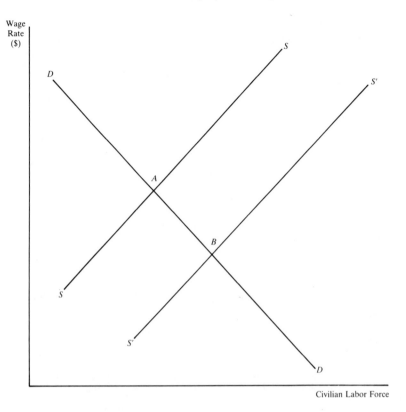

**Figure 5–2.** Wages and the Labor Force

where *Ns* is the number of units supplied of labor and *Nd* is the number of units demanded of labor.

It follows from conventional theory that

$$\partial W/\partial Ns < 0 \qquad\qquad (5.8)$$

and

$$\partial W/\partial Nd > 0. \qquad\qquad (5.9)$$

The rate of change of money wages over time is then described by a general implicit function such as

$$dW/dt = f\,[(dNs/dt,\ dNd/dt)] \qquad\qquad (5.10)$$

where $t$ is time.

The restrictions imposed on the partial derivatives in equation 5.10 are as follows:

$$\frac{\partial f}{\partial(dNs/dt)} < 0 \qquad (5.11)$$

and

$$\frac{\partial f}{\partial(dNd/dt)} > 0. \qquad (5.12)$$

It follows from equations 5.11 and 5.12 that

$$dW/dt \gtreqless 0 \text{ as } dNd/dt \gtreqless dNs/dt. \qquad (5.13)$$

Moreover, from equations 5.11 and 5.13 it may be inferred that the greater the net in-migration rate to an area, the slower the rate of increase in that area's money-wage rates.

The inverse relationship between the rate of increase in money-wage rates and the net in-migration rate is illustrated in figure 5–3. The curve shown in figure 5–3 looks very much like, and actually is analytically similar to, the traditional Phillips curve.[3] Moreover, such a curve has been, in principle, empirically confirmed in a two-stage least-squares-regression analysis by Cebula and Vedder (1976).

A reduction in the rate of change (increase) in money wages tends to reduce the rate of change (increase) in total production costs. In turn, a reduced rate of increase in total production costs tends to lead to a diminished rate of increase in final commodity prices. Obviously, the more competitive the business environment, the greater the degree to which the regional inflation rate will respond to reductions in the growth rates of production costs. In any event, it is argued here that the greater the net in-migration rate to an area, the lower the regional inflation rate. Figure 5–1 conveniently depicts this relationship between regional inflation rates and rates of net in-migration.[4]

*The Impact of Per-Capita-Income Growth Rates*

Here it is argued that, all else being equal (ceteris paribus), the regional inflation rate depends directly on the rate of growth of per-capita income.

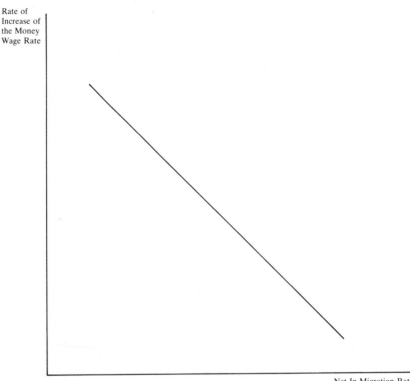

**Figure 5–3.**  Wages and Migration

As a region's per-capita income grows, so too does the aggregate demand for goods and services within the region. Other things held the same, as the region's aggregate demand grows over time, the inflation rate within the region rises because of the forces of excess demand. The more rapid the growth rate in per-capita income, the more rapid the growth rate of aggregate commodity demand and thus the more rapid the rate of inflation.

The aggregate demand for commodities within a region may be described by the following implicit function:

$$Di = Di \ (Ci, \ Ii, \ \ldots) \tag{5.14}$$

where

$Di$ is the aggregate commodity demand in region $i$;

$Ci$ is the aggregate price (living-cost) level in region $i$; and

$Ii$ is the per-capita income level in region $i$.

In accord with conventional theory, it is expected that

$$\partial Di/\partial Ci < 0, \text{ and } \partial Di/\partial Ii > 0. \tag{5.15}$$

The aggregate supply of commodities in the region presumably may be described by

$$Si = Si\ (Ci,\ \ldots) \tag{5.16}$$

where $Si$ is the aggregate supply of commodities in region $i$.

According to orthodox theory, it is expected that

$$\partial Si/\partial Ci > 0. \tag{5.17}$$

In the very short run, it may be that

$$\partial Si/\partial Ci = 0. \tag{5.18}$$

In order to avoid the possibility of constructing a Marshallian or Walrasian unstable system, we reject the possibility that[5]

$$\partial Si/\partial Ci < 0. \tag{5.19}$$

For convenience, we also reject the possibility represented in equation 5.18.
    From equations 5.14 and 5.15, it follows that the growth in aggregate commodity demand over time is described by

$$dDi/dt = g\ (dCi/dt,\ dIi/dt,\ \ldots) \tag{5.20}$$

where $t$ is time

From equations 5.15 and 5.20 it logically follows that

$$\frac{\partial(dDi/dt)}{\partial(dIi/dt)} > 0. \tag{5.21}$$

Thus, the more rapid the growth rate over time of a region's per-capita income, the more rapid the growth rate of its aggregate commodity demand.
    Assuming a dynamically stable system, a positive rate of growth in per-capita income in region $i$ will elicit growth in region $i$'s aggregate

commodity demand and hence a higher inflation rate in region $i$ so long as either of the two following sets of conditions prevails:[6]

$$dSi/dt = 0, \ dDi/dt > 0 \qquad (5.22)$$

or

$$dSi/dt > 0, \ dDi/dt > 0, \ dDi/dt > dSi/dt. \qquad (5.23)$$

In conclusion, then, especially under an assumption of ceteris paribus,[7] it follows that the inflation rate in a region is an increasing function over time of the growth rate of per-capita income within the region.[8] This hypothesized relationship is represented in figure 5–4.

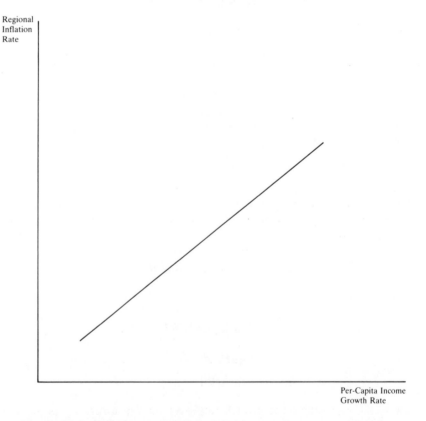

**Figure 5–4.** Inflationary Effects of Growth in Per-Capita Income

*Inflationary Effects of Unionization Growth Rates*

Here it is argued that the regional inflation rate is an increasing function of the rate of growth of the percentage of a region's civilian labor force that is unionized. Presumably, the higher the percentage of a region's civilian labor force that is unionized, the greater the upward pressure on the "wage package."[9] And the higher the average wage package in a region, the higher the overall final-output-price structure in the region. When put into a dynamic context, it can be concluded that the more rapid the unionization growth rate in a region, the higher the inflation rate in the region, all else equal.

We begin with the following simple proposition:

$$PNi = PNi \, (Ui, \, . \, . \, .) \qquad (5.24)$$

where

> $PNi$ is the wage package in region $i$ (in other words, the average hourly money-wage rate plus all fringe benefits prorated on an hourly basis, in region $i$); and

> $Ui$ is the unionization rate in region $i$ (in other words, the percentage of the civilian labor force in region $i$ that is unionized).

It is argued here that

$$\partial PNi / \partial Ui > 0. \qquad (5.25)$$

This conforms to the related arguments developed in chapter 4.

The total costs of production for representative firm $j$ in region $i$ is given by

$$Lij = PNij + Oij \qquad (5.26)$$

where

> $Lij$ is the total production costs for firm $j$ in region $i$;

> $PNij$ is the wage package for firm $j$ in region $i$; and

> $Oij$ is all other production costs facing firm $j$ in region $i$.

Clearly, from equation 5.26 it follows that

$$Lij = Lij \ (PNj, \ Oij). \tag{5.27}$$

In addition, it follows logically that[10]

$$\partial Lij/\partial PNj > 0. \tag{5.28}$$

From equations 5.25 and 5.28, it may reasonably be inferred that[11]

$$\partial Lij/\partial Ui > 0. \tag{5.29}$$

From this it is in turn reasonable to argue that final commodity prices are also a direct function of $Ui$. Put into a dynamic context, it may be further inferred that the inflation rate of final commodity prices in a region is an increasing function of the rate of growth of the unionization rate in the region. This may be stated mathematically as

$$\partial^2 Ci/\partial Ui^2 > 0 \tag{5.30}$$

where $Ci$ is the aggregate price (living-cost) level in region $i$.

The relationship represented in 5.30 is graphically depicted in figure 5–5.

*Inflationary Effects of Taxation Growth Rates*

The level of state and local taxation in a region theoretically may influence the overall living-cost level in both *direct* and *indirect* ways. Because of this it may be inferred that the inflation rate in a region is an increasing function of the growth rate of state plus local taxation levels.

The consumer seeks to maximize his utility subject to a budget constraint of the following general form:

$$Y = \sum_{v=1}^{n} PvXv + TT \tag{5.31}$$

where

$Y$ is the individual's gross income level;

$Pv$ is unit price of pure private good $v$; $v = 1, \ldots, n$;

$Xv$ is the number of units consumed by the individual of pure private good $v$; $v = 1, \ldots, n$; and

$TT$ is the individual's total tax burden.

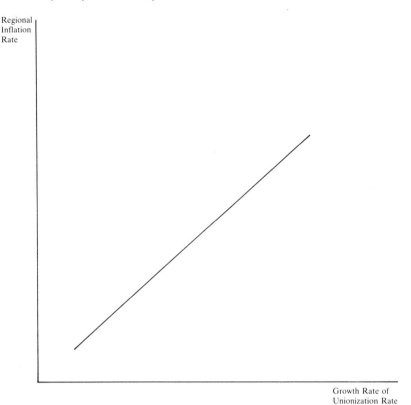

**Figure 5–5.** Inflationary Effects of Growth in the Unionization Rate

The term *TT* can be broken down as follows:

$$TT = TF + TN \tag{5.32}$$

where *TF* is the individual's federal tax liability and *TN* is the individual's state plus local tax liability.

Substituting from equation 5.32 into equation 5.31 yields

$$Y = \sum_{v=1}^{n} PvXv + TF + TN. \tag{5.33}$$

From equation 5.33 it may be inferred that the consumer's gross outlay (expenditures) are given by

$$H = \sum_{v=1}^{n} PvXv + TF + TN \qquad (5.34)$$

where $H$ is the consumer's total outlay (expenditures).

The following outlay function may be derived from equation 5.34:

$$H = H\ (P_1,\ \ldots\ ,\ Pn,\ x_1,\ \ldots\ ,\ Xn,\ TF,\ TN). \qquad (5.35)$$

It follows logically that

$$\partial H/\partial TN > 0. \qquad (5.36)$$

Thus, higher state plus local taxation levels *directly* raise the individual's overall outlay (living costs). Stated in a dynamic context, it follows that the rate of growth of the cost of living is an increasing function of the rate of growth of the state plus local taxation level, all else held the same.

The analysis in equations 5.31 through 5.36 argues that there is a *direct* impact of the growth rate of state plus local taxation levels on the regional inflation rate. The *indirect* impact of the growth rate of state plus local taxation levels on regional inflation rates involves the cost functions of producers (firms). The profit-maximizing firm seeks to minimize the level of its production costs at every output level. To the extent that state plus local taxes, such as property taxes, are included in the firm's production costs, higher levels of such taxes raise the firm's long-run total production costs. As a result of higher production costs, in the long run, final output prices are higher.[12] Put into a dynamic context, it is argued here that the greater the growth rate of state plus local taxation levels, the greater the regional inflation rate in the long run.[13]

Figure 5–6 illustrates the relationship between regional inflation rates and the growth rate of state plus local taxation levels. The relationship is of course a direct one. Moreover, the magnitude of the slope of the line in figure 5–6 depends on both the direct *and* indirect inflationary impacts of the rate of growth of state plus local government taxation.

**Empirical Analysis**

It has been argued here that the regional inflation rate depends in part upon the net in-migration rate, the growth rate of per-capita income, the growth rate of the unionization rate of the civilian labor force, and the growth rate of per-capita state plus local taxation levels. These hypotheses will be tested

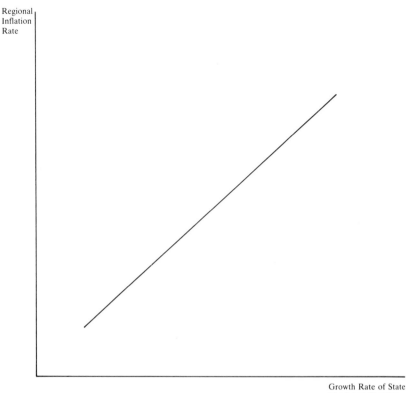

**Figure 5–6.** Inflation and Taxation

using conventional multiple-linear-regression analysis. Three different empirical specifications will be presented and analyzed.

Based on the four hypotheses, the following model is postulated:

$$\Delta Ci = \Delta Ci \ (Mi, \ \Delta Ii, \ \Delta Ui, \ \Delta TXi) \qquad (5.37)$$

where

$\Delta Ci$ is a measure of the inflation rate in region $i$;

$Mi$ is a measure of net in-migration to region $i$;

$\Delta Ii$ is a measure of the growth rate of per-capita income in region $i$;

$\Delta Ui$ is a measure of the growth rate of the unionization rate in region $i$; and

$\Delta TXi$ is a measure of the growth rate of per-capita state plus local taxation levels in region $i$.

The expected signs of the partial derivatives in equation 5.37 are as follows

$$\partial(\Delta Ci)/\partial Mi < 0 \qquad\qquad (5.38)$$

$$\partial(\Delta Ci)/\partial(\Delta Ii) > 0 \qquad\qquad (5.39)$$

$$\partial(\Delta Ci)/\partial(\Delta Ui) > 0 \qquad\qquad (5.40)$$

$$\partial(\Delta Ci)/\partial(\Delta TXi) > 0. \qquad\qquad (5.41)$$

The signs exhibited in equations 5.38 through 5.41 derive directly from the theoretical analysis in the preceding section of this chapter.

The actual regression equation to be estimated is given by

$$\Delta Ci = d_0 + d_1 Mi + d_2 \Delta Ii + d_3 \Delta Ui + d_4 \Delta TXi + \mu \qquad (5.42)$$

where

$\Delta Ci$ is the percentage rate of growth of the average annual cost of living for a four-person family living on an intermediate budget in SMSA $i$, 1970–1978;

$d_0$ is a constant term;

$Mi$ is the net in-migration rate to SMSA $i$, 1970–1978;[14]

$\Delta Ii$ is the percentage rate of growth of the per-capita income level in SMSA $i$, 1970–1978;

$\Delta Ui$ is the percentage rate of growth of the unionization rate in SMSA $i$, 1970–1978;

$\Delta TXi$ is the percentage rate of growth of the per-capita state plus local taxation level in SMSA $i$, 1970–1978; and

$\mu$ is a stochastic-error term.

It is mathematically possible that[15]

$$\Delta Ci \gtrless 0, \ Mi \gtrless 0, \ \Delta Ii \gtrless 0, \ \Delta Ui \gtrless 0, \ \text{or} \ \Delta TXi \gtrless 0. \qquad (5.43)$$

In point of fact, there are several cases where $Mi > 0$ and $Mi < 0$. For this reason, the regression equation in 5.42 must be linear as opposed to log-linear.[16]

The expected signs on the linear coefficients in regression equation 5.42 are as follows:

$$\partial(\Delta Ci)/\partial Mi = d_1 < 0 \tag{5.44}$$

$$\partial(\Delta Ci)/\partial(\Delta Ii) = d_2 > 0 \tag{5.45}$$

$$\partial(\Delta Ci)/\partial(\Delta Ui) = d_3 > 0 \tag{5.46}$$

$$\partial(\Delta Ci)/\partial(\Delta TXi) = d_4 > 0. \tag{5.47}$$

Sufficient data were available to estimate regression equation 5.42 for some thirty-six SMSAs. In all, there are five estimators in equation 5.42 ($d_0$, $d_1$, $d_2$, $d_3$, and $d_4$). Hence, the regression estimate will have a total of 31 degrees of freedom ($DF$).

The ordinary least-squares estimate of regression equation 5.42 is given by

$$\Delta Ci = +5.56000 - 0.10286Mi + 0.20739\Delta Ii$$
$$(+8.14) \qquad (-1.56) \qquad (+2.65)$$

$$+ 0.26251\Delta Ui + 0.09085\Delta TXi$$
$$(+3.35) \qquad (+2.37)$$

$$R^2 = 0.38 \qquad \langle R \rangle_{av}^2 = 0.30 \qquad n = 36 \qquad DF = 31$$

$$F = 4.78505 \tag{5.48}$$

where the terms in the parentheses beneath the coefficients are signed $t$-values.

In regression estimate 5.48, all four of the estimated coefficients have the hypothesized signs. In addition, three of the four estimated coefficients (those for the variables $\Delta Ii$, $\Delta Ui$, and $\Delta TXi$) are statistically significant at the 0.01 level or better. In addition, the estimated coefficient for the fourth exogenous variable ($Mi$) is statistically significant at approximately the 0.10 level. The $R^2$ is 0.38 and the $\langle R \rangle_{av}^2$ is 0.30; hence, the model explains approximately one-third of the variation in the endogenous inflation-rate variable. The $F$-ratio is statistically significant at nearly the 0.05 level.

Scanning the zero-order correlation coefficients among the independent variables in equation 5.48 reveals that there are no major multicollinearity problems. In equation 5.48, the only estimated coefficient that is not statistically significant is that for the migration variable. The zero-order correlation coefficients between the variable $Mi$ and the other exogenous variables ($\Delta Ii$, $\Delta Ui$, and $\Delta TXi$) in the analysis are:

1.  $Mi$ and $\Delta Ii$, at $+0.39$;
2.  $Mi$ and $\Delta Ui$, at $-0.30$; and
3.  $Mi$ and $\Delta TXi$, at $+0.43$.

Although the variable $Mi$ is somewhat correlated with all three of the other independent variables, in no case is the degree of correlation especially high. Consequently, the failure of the estimated coefficient of the migration variable to be statistically significant at the 0.01 level is not genuinely attributable to multicollinearity.

An examination of the results shown in regression equation 5.48 reveals that the migration variable worked as hypothesized but that it was rather weak. Thus, empirical estimate 5.48 provides only modest support for the migration/regional-inflation-rate hypothesis. However, the estimated coefficient of the variable for per-capita income growth rate is statistically significant at the 0.01 level. Thus, it appears that the regional inflation rate is an increasing function of the rate of growth of a region's per-capita income level. The estimated coefficient of the unionization-growth-rate variable is statistically significant at well beyond the 0.01 level. It appears that the inflation rate within a region is an increasing function of the rate of growth of the unionization rate of the civilian labor force within the region. Finally, the findings in regression estimate 5.48 indicate that the estimated coefficient of the tax-growth variable is statistically significant at roughly the 0.01 level. Therefore, it would appear that the rate of inflation within a given region is directly a function of the rate of growth of per-capita state plus local taxation levels within the region, ceteris paribus.

Overall, the results in regression estimate 5.48 provide very strong empirical support for the four hypotheses developed earlier in this chapter. Nevertheless, the estimated coefficients of one variable, the net in-migration rate, is only marginally significant.[17] Accordingly, following standard econometric practice, the following alternative to regression equation 5.42 is estimated:[18]

$$\Delta Ci = e_0 + e_1 \Delta Ii + e_2 \Delta Ui + e_3 \Delta TXi + e \qquad (5.49)$$

where

$\Delta Ci$, $\Delta Ii$, $\Delta Ui$, and $\Delta TXi$ are as in equation 5.37;

$e_0$ is a constant term; and

$e$ is a stochastic-error term.

In the empirical estimation of equation 5.49, there were some thirty-six data points. The SMSAs examined in equation 5.49 are identical to those examined in equation 5.42.

In accord with the hypotheses stated earlier in this chapter, it follows that we should expect:

$$\partial(\Delta Ci)/\partial(\Delta Ii) = e_1 > 0 \tag{5.50}$$

$$\partial(\Delta Ci)/\partial(\Delta Ui) = e_2 > 0 \tag{5.51}$$

$$\partial(\Delta Ci)/\partial(\Delta TXi) = e_3 > 0 \tag{5.52}$$

where $e_1$, $e_2$, and $e_3$ are the linear coefficients from regression equation 5.49.

The ordinary least-squares estimate of regression equation 5.49 is given by

$$\Delta Ci = +5.92056 + 0.17694\Delta Ii$$
$$(+9.01) \qquad (+2.29)$$

$$+ \ 0.27545\Delta Ui + 0.06949\Delta TXi$$
$$(+3.46) \qquad\qquad (+1.89)$$

$$R^2 = 0.33 \qquad \langle R \rangle_{av}^2 = 0.27 \qquad n = 36 \qquad DF = 32$$

$$F = 5.33335 \tag{5.53}$$

where the terms in the parentheses are $t$-values.

In regression estimate 5.53, all three of the estimated coefficients exhibited the expected signs.[19] In addition, two of the three estimated coefficients (those for the variables $\Delta Ii$ and $\Delta Ui$) were statistically significant at the 0.01 level or beyond. The third coefficient (that corresponding to the variable $\Delta TXi$) is statistically significant at nearly the 0.05 level. The $R^2$ is 0.33 and the $\langle R \rangle_{av}^2$ is 0.27; consequently, the model explains roughly three-tenths of the variation in the regional inflation rate. The $F$-ratio is statistically significant at nearly the 0.05 level in equation 5.53.

There were no major multicollinearity problems among the exogenous variables in regression estimate 5.53. The zero-order correlation coefficients between the variable $\Delta TXi$ and the other two exogenous variables in the system are $\Delta TXi$ and $\Delta Ii$, at $+0.28$; and $\Delta TXi$ and $\Delta Ui$, at $-0.24$. These two cases of statistical correlation are relatively minor. As a result, the relative weakness of the coefficient of the exogenous variable $\Delta TXi$ in regression equation 5.53 is not realistically attributable to multicollinearity.[20]

On the basis of regression estimate 5.53, it appears that the regional inflation rate is an increasing function of the rate of growth of regional per-capita income. This result is very similar to that found in regression equation 5.48. The coefficient of the unionization-growth-rate variable is highly significant in equation 5.53. Thus, the regional inflation rate would appear to be a direct function of the growth of the unionization rate of the civilian labor force within a region. This result is entirely compatible with the finding in regression estimate 5.48. Finally, the coefficient of the tax-growth variable in regression equation 5.53 is statistically significant at approximately the 0.05 level. Thus, there appears to be moderately convincing evidence that the regional inflation rate is an increasing function of the regional growth rate of per-capita state plus local taxation levels. The tax-growth variable was considerably stronger in regression estimate 5.48 than in equation 5.53.

A comparison of regression estimates 5.48 and 5.53 reveals two very obvious differences:

1.  the presence of variable $Mi$ in equation 5.48 and the absence of variable $Mi$ in equation 5.53; and
2.  a distinctly lower $t$-value of the coefficient for the variable $\Delta TXi$ in equation 5.53 than was the case in equation 5.48.

Other differences between regression equation 5.48 and 5.53 are also rather apparent. For example, the $R^2$ and $\langle R \rangle_{av}^2$ values are both distinctly higher in equation 5.48 than in equation 5.53.

In an effort to improve upon the regression results in equations 5.48 and 5.53, the variable $Mi$ is now to be replaced by a broader category of population variable, $\Delta Popi$. The variable $\Delta Popi$ is defined here as the percentage rate of growth of the total population in SMSA $i$, 1970–1978. This new variable includes both net in-migration and the net natural increase in the population.[21] Since the variable $\Delta Popi$ is a replacement for the variable $Mi$, it is expected here that the regional inflation rate is a decreasing function of the growth rate of the total population.[22]

The general model to be examined now takes the following form:

$$\Delta Ci = \Delta Ci\ (\Delta Popi,\ \Delta Ii,\ \Delta Ui,\ \Delta TXi) \qquad (5.54)$$

where $\Delta Ci$, $\Delta Popi$, $\Delta Ii$, $\Delta Ui$, and $\Delta TXi$ are as in equation 5.42.

The expected signs of the partial derivatives in equation 5.54 are as follows:

$$\partial(\Delta Ci)/\partial(\Delta Popi) < 0 \tag{5.55}$$

$$\partial(\Delta Ci)/\partial(\Delta Ii) > 0 \tag{5.56}$$

$$\partial(\Delta Ci)/\partial(\Delta Ui) > 0 \tag{5.57}$$

$$\partial(\Delta Ci)/\partial(\Delta TXi) > 0. \tag{5.58}$$

The actual regression equation to be estimated is given by

$$\Delta Ci = f_0 + f_1\Delta Popi + f_2\Delta Ii + f_3\Delta Ui + f_4\Delta TXi + f \tag{5.59}$$

where $f_0$ is a constant term and $f$ is a stochastic-error term.

It follows from equations 5.54, 5.55, and 5.59 that

$$\partial(\Delta Ci)/\partial(\Delta Popi) = f_1. \tag{5.60}$$

Accordingly, the expected signs of the various linear coefficients in regression equation 5.59 are

$$f_1 < 0, \ f_2 > 0, \ f_3 > 0, \ \text{and} \ f_4 > 0. \tag{5.61}$$

The ordinary least-squares estimate of regression equation 5.59 is given by

$$\Delta Ci = +5.73066 - 5.68727\Delta Popi + 0.19554\Delta Ii$$
$$(+8.01) \qquad (-0.71) \qquad\qquad (+2.38)$$

$$+ \ 0.26860\Delta Ui + 0.08358\Delta TXi$$
$$(+3.33) \qquad\qquad (+1.99)$$

$$R^2 = 0.34 \qquad \langle R\rangle_{av}^2 = 0.26 \qquad n = 36 \qquad DF = 31$$

$$F = 4.06145 \tag{5.62}$$

where terms in parentheses are $t$-values.

In regression equation 5.62, all four of the estimated coefficients have the predicted signs. The estimated coefficients of two variables ($\Delta Ii$ and

$\Delta Ui$) are both statistically significant at beyond the 0.01 level, whereas the estimated coefficient of a third variable ($\Delta TXi$) is statistically significant at the 0.05 level. Only the estimated coefficient of the new variable, $\Delta Popi$, fails to be statistically significant at an acceptable level.[23] The $R^2$ is 0.34 and the $\langle R \rangle_{av}^2$ is 0.26, so that the model explains roughly three-tenths to one-third of the variation in the regional inflation rate. The $F$-ratio is not quite statistically significant at the 0.05 level.

A review of the zero-order correlation coefficients among the exogenous variables in regression estimate 5.62 revealed the following single case of multicollinearity: $\Delta Popi$ and $\Delta TXi$, at +0.54. This particular instance of multicollinearity may in part account for the weakness of both of the involved exogenous variables in regression equation 5.62. The magnitude of the correlation coefficient is too low, however, for one to attribute *all* of the observed weakness of the variable $\Delta Popi$ to multicollinearity.

In equation 5.62, the estimated coefficient of the new variable, $\Delta Popi$, is not statistically significant at any acceptable level. Thus, the variable $\Delta Popi$ does not explain regional inflation rates in a significant way. The estimated coefficient of the variable $\Delta Ii$ is statistically significant at the 0.01 level.

Hence, it appears that the regional inflation rate is an increasing function of the growth rate of a region's per-capita income level. This finding is consistent with the results in regression equations 5.48 and 5.53. The unionization growth rate is also statistically significant at the 0.01 level. Thus, the regional inflation rate is an increasing function of the growth rate of the unionization rate of a region's civilian labor force. Equations 5.48 and 5.53 both generated the same conclusion regarding the exogenous variable $\Delta Ui$.

Finally, the estimated coefficent of the tax-growth variable is statistically significant at the 0.05 level. This result implies that the regional inflation rate is an increasing function of the per-capita growth rate of state plus local taxation levels.[24] Equations 5.48 and 5.53 yielded very much the same conclusion regarding the variable $\Delta TXi$.

**Summary and Conclusions**

Earlier in this book, four sets of hypotheses regarding the determinants of geographic *living-cost* levels and geographic *living-cost* differentials were developed (chapter 2). The present chapter shifts emphasis from a static analysis of regional *living-cost levels* to a more dynamic analysis of regional *inflation rates*. It has been hypothesized in this chapter that the regional inflation rate is a decreasing function of the rate of net in-migration; the regional inflation rate is an increasing function of the growth rate of per-capita income levels; the regional inflation rate is an increasing function of the growth rate of the unionization rate of the civilian labor force; and the regional inflation rate is an increasing function of the growth rate of per-capita state plus local taxation levels. The first of these four hypotheses received only minor empirical support. However, the last three hypotheses all received very strong empirical support in three different sets of regression estimates.

Chapter 6 will address in detail the economic and public-policy implications of the limitations of this study.

## Notes

1. Related to this issue, see the studies by Cebula (1979 and 1981), Renas and Kumar (1978, 1979, and 1981), Alperovich (1979), and Rabianski (1971). See also the somewhat different but related studies by Fields (1976) and Cebula (1978).

2. Of course, the more competitive the business environment, the greater the degree to which the dynamic agglomeration economies will succeed in reducing regional inflation rates.

3. Related to this topic, see Phillips (1958). Concerning the idea of a regional Phillips curve (relation), see also Marcis and Reed (1974), Reed and Hutchinson (1976), and Hutchinson and Reed (1978).

4. The relationship shown in figure 5–1 derives from two sets of influences.

5. Related to the stability issue, see Bilas (1967) and Henderson and Quandt (1958).

6. Actually, the upward price pressure over time also can be manifested if $dSi/dt < 0$, $dDi/dt = 0$. Other such combinations of conditions are possible as well. For example, consider the following case: $dSi/dt < 0$, $dDi/dt > 0$.

7. All else equal, in this instance it follows that $dSi/dt = 0$.

8. Thus, it is argued here that the following obtains: $(\partial^2 Ci)/(\partial Ii^2) > 0$.

9. The wage package includes wages per se plus fringe benefits.

10. Obviously, it is also true that $(\partial Lij)/(\partial Oij) > 0$.

11. The argument in equation 5.29 is based on the following: $Lij = Lij$ $(PNj, Oij) = Lij [PNj (Ui, \ldots), Oij]$.

12. The degree to which final output prices rise will naturally depend on the degree of competitiveness in the business environment within the region in question.

13. The strength of this inflationary impact is increased by the extent to which rising taxes lead to increased labor intensity in the production process.

14. The variable $Mi$ is expressed as a decimal and is computed as follows:

$$Mi = \frac{\text{net number of in-migrants to SMSA } i, \ 1970-1978}{1970 \text{ total population in SMSA } i}.$$

15. Indeed, it is also possible that $\Delta Ci = 0$, $Mi = 0$, $\Delta Ii = 0$, $\Delta Ui = 0$, or $\Delta TXi = 0$.

16. Recall that a log-linear specification cannot deal with negative numbers. Related to this issue, see, for example, Dhrymes (1970), Johnston (1972), Theil (1971), or Bridge (1971).

17. Ideally, the coefficient of the variable $Mi$ should have been statistically significant at the 0.05 level or better. Unfortunately, the findings in equation 5.48 indicate a statistical significance at only the 0.10 level.

18. Related to this standard econometric practice, see Theil (1971), Bridge (1971), Dhrymes (1970), or Johnston (1972).

19. These signs are indicated in inequalities 5.50 through 5.52.

20. Usually, multicollinearity is thought to be a possible problem only if the zero-order correlation coefficient is greater than +0.50 or less than −0.50. Related to this issue, see Theil (1971), Bridge (1971), Dhrymes (1970), or Johnston (1972).

21. The net natural increase in the population is the number of births minus the number of deaths.

22. Related to this hypothesis, see Isard (1956) or Nourse (1968).

23. In point of fact, the estimated coefficient of the variable $\Delta Popi$ is not statistically significant at even the 0.20 level.

24. This finding may yield interesting public-policy implications. Related to this possibility, see Cebula and Chevlin (1981).

## References

Alperovich, G. 1979. "The Cost of Living, Labor Market Opportunities and the Migration Decision: A Case of Misspecification?: Comment." *Annals of Regional Science* 13: 102–105.

Bilas, R.A. 1967. *Microeconomic Theory: A Graphical Analysis*. New York: McGraw-Hill.

Bridge, J.L. 1971. *Applied Econometrics*. New York: North-Holland.

———. 1978. "An Empirical Note on the Tiebout-Tullock Hypothesis." *Quarterly Journal of Economics* 93:705–711.

———. 1979. *The Determinants of Human Migration*. Lexington, Mass.: D.C. Heath, Lexington Books.

Cebula, R.J. 1981. "The Cost of Living, Labor Market Opportunities and the Migration Decision: A Case of Misspecification?—A Comment," *Annals of Regional Science* 15:73–74.

Cebula, R.J., and Chevlin, L. 1981. "Proposition 4, Tax Reduction Mirage:

An Exploratory Note on its Potential Spending and Tax Impacts." *American Journal of Economics and Sociology* 40:343–348.

Cebula, R.J., and Vedder, R.K. 1976. "Migration, Economic Opportunity, and the Quality of Life: Reply and Extension." *Journal of Regional Science* 16:113–116.

Dhrymes, P.J. 1970. *Econometrics: Statistical Foundations and Applications*. New York: Harper and Row.

Fields, G.S. 1976. "Labor Force Migration, Unemployment and Job Turnover." *Review of Economics and Statistics* 58:407–415.

Henderson, J.M., and Quandt, R.E. 1958. *Microeconomic Theory: A Mathematical Approach*. New York: McGraw-Hill.

Hutchinson, P.M., and Reed, J.D. 1978. "An Empirical Test of a Regional Phillips Curve and Wage Rate Transmission Mechanism in an Urban Hierarchy: Reply." *Annals of Regional Science* 12:100–103.

Isard, W. 1956. *Location and Space Economy*. Cambridge, Mass.: MIT Press.

Johnston, J. 1972. *Econometric Methods*. New York: McGraw-Hill.

Marcis, R.G., and Reed, J.D. 1974. "Joint Estimation of the Determinants of Wages in Subregional Labor Markets in the United States: 1961–1972." *Journal of Regional Science* 14:259–267.

Nourse, H. 1968. *Regional Economics*. New York: McGraw-Hill.

Phillips, A.W. 1958. "The Relation between Unemployment and the Rate of Change of Money Wage Rates in the United Kingdom, 1861–1957." *Economica* 25:283–299.

Rabianski, J.S. 1971. "Real Earnings and Human Migration." *Journal of Human Resources* 6:185–192.

Reed, J.D., and Hutchinson, P.M. 1976. "An Empirical Test of a Regional Phillips Curve and Wage Rate Transmission Mechanism in an Urban Hierarchy." *Annals of Regional Science* 10:19–30.

Renas, S.M., and Kumar, R. 1978. "The Cost of Living, Labor Market Opportunities, and the Migration Decision: A Case of Misspecification?" *Annals of Regional Science* 12:95–104.

———. 1979. "The Cost of Living, Labor Market Opportunities and the Migration Decision: A Case of Misspecification?: Reply." *Annals of Regional Science* 13:106–108.

———. 1981. "The Cost of Living, Labor Market Opportunities, and the Migration Decision: Some Additional Evidence." *Annals of Regional Science* 15:74–79.

Theil, H. 1971. *Principles of Econometrics*. New York: Wiley.

**Part IV
Summary**

# 6

# Overview and Conclusions

Chapter 6 has four basic objectives. First, it seeks to provide further insights into the determinants of living-cost differentials by focusing on the cost of *housing* rather than on the *overall* cost of living. Second, it seeks to summarize the principal empirical findings of this book. Third, it seeks to discuss in detail some of the theoretical and empirical limitations of this study. Fourth, it seeks to analyze the economic and public-policy implications of the study.

## The Cost of Housing

In the first five chapters of this book, the emphasis has been on the *overall* level of the cost of living in metropolitan areas. Efforts have been to explain the determinants of the *overall* level of the cost of living, the determinants of geographic differentials in *overall* living-cost levels, and to explain the rate of change over time in the *overall* cost of living. Here an alternative measure of living-cost differentials is considered: the *cost of housing*. Because of the magnitude of the monetary cost of housing in the typical American family's annual and lifetime budget, such a change in the manner of measuring living costs is not at all unreasonable; indeed, such a change may be very appropriate and desirable. To investigate the determinants of the cost of housing in metropolitan areas, a linear-regression model will be estimated by ordinary least squares for 1967, 1972, 1975, 1978, and 1979.

The basic model developed in chapters 2 and 3 is given by

$$C_i = C_i \ (P_i, \ D_i, \ I_i, \ R_i) \qquad (6.1)$$

where

$C_i$ is the average annual cost of living (*all items*) for a four-person family living in SMSA $i$ on an intermediate budget;

$P_i$ is the total population in SMSA $i$;

$D_i$ is the population density in SMSA $i$ in terms of the number of persons per square mile;

$I_i$ is the per-capita income level in SMSA $i$; and

167

$Ri$ is a dummy variable to indicate the presence of right-to-work legislation in the state where SMSA $i$ is principally located.

As noted in chapter 3, the following obtains:

$$Ri = 0 \text{ or } Ri = 1. \tag{6.2}$$

On the basis of the arguments in chapter 2, it is expected that

$$\partial Ci/\partial Pi < 0 \tag{6.3}$$

$$\partial Ci/\partial Di > 0 \tag{6.4}$$

$$\partial Ci/\partial Ii > 0 \tag{6.5}$$

$$\partial Ci/\partial Ri < 0. \tag{6.6}$$

The actual regression equation that was estimated by ordinary least squares in chapter 3 is of the following general form:

$$Ci = a_0 + a_1 Pi + a_2 Di + a_3 Ii + a_4 Ri + \mu \tag{6.7}$$

where $a_0$ is a constant term and $\mu$ is a stochastic-error term.

Equations of the form given in 6.7 were estimated in chapter 3 for the *overall* cost of living for all of the fourteen years from 1966 through 1979. Now, the average annual cost of *housing* is to be the dependent variable. The general form of the model is now given by

$$Zi = Ai \ (Pi, \ Di, \ Ii, \ Ri) \tag{6.8}$$

where $Zi$ is the average annual cost of housing for a four-person family living in SMSA $i$ on an intermediate budget; and $Pi$, $Di$, $Ii$, and $Ri$ are as in equation 6.1.

Since the nature of the variable $Ci$ is comprehensive, whereas the nature of the variable $Zi$ is restricted to housing, it follows that

$$Zi < Ci \text{ for all } i. \tag{6.9}$$

The cost of housing in any given metropolitan area, $Zi$, includes the weighted average total cost of shelter for renters and homeowners (inclusive of interest and taxes where applicable), home furnishings, and normal household repairs and operations. The data are compiled annually by the U.S. Bureau of Labor Statistics. These data are available for some thirty-nine SMSAs from 1966 through 1978; for the year 1979 and thereafter, these data are available for only twenty-four SMSAs. The housing-cost data are, to a reasonable extent, geographically comparable.

The actual form of the regression equation to be estimated for the cost of housing is given by

$$Zit = b_0t + b_1tPit + b_2tDit + b_3tIit + b_4tRit + \mu t \qquad (6.10)$$

where

$Zit$ is the average annual total cost of housing for a four-person family living in SMSA $i$ on an intermediate budget during year $t$;

$b_0t$ is a constant term for year $t$;

$Pit$ is the total population in SMSA $i$ during year $t$;

$Dit$ is the population density in SMSA $i$ during year $t$, expressed in terms of the number of persons per square mile;

$Iit$ is the per-capita income level in SMSA $i$ during year $t$;

$Rit$ is a dummy variable used to indicate the presence of right-to-work legislation in SMSA $i$ during year $t$;[1] and

$\mu t$ is a stochastic-error term, year $t$.

The model expressed in equations 6.8 and 6.10 is analytically identical to that expressed in equations 6.1 and 6.7 except for the substitution of the housing-cost variable $Zi$ for the overall living-cost variable $Ci$.[2] Accordingly, it follows from equations 6.3 through 6.6 that

$$\partial Zit/\partial Pit = b_1t < 0 \qquad (6.11)$$

$$\partial Zit/\partial Dit = b_2t > 0 \qquad (6.12)$$

$$\partial Zit/\partial Iit = b_3t > 0 \qquad (6.13)$$

$$\partial Zit/\partial Rit = b_4t < 0. \qquad (6.14)$$

The model in equation 6.10 is to be estimated for 1967, 1972, 1975, 1978, and 1979. Hence, the value of $t$ in equations 6.10 through 6.14 is given by

$$t = 1967, \ 1972, \ 1975, \ 1978, \ \text{and} \ 1979. \qquad (6.15)$$

These five years were chosen entirely at random. Estimating regression equation 6.10 for other years in the period from 1966 through 1979 yields the same essential overall findings as obtained for the years listed in equation 6.15.

For the years 1967, 1972, 1975, and 1978, there were sufficient data available for the analysis of thirty-nine metropolitan areas: Atlanta, Ga.; Austin, Tex.; Bakersfield, Cal.; Baltimore, Md.; Baton Rouge, La.; Boston, Mass.; Buffalo, N.Y.; Cedar Rapids, Iowa; Champaign-Urbana, Ill.; Chicago, Ill.; Cincinnati, Ohio; Cleveland, Ohio; Dallas, Tex.; Dayton, Ohio; Denver, Col.; Detroit, Mich.; Durham, N.C.; Green Bay, Wis.; Hartford, Conn.; Honolulu, Hawaii; Houston, Tex.; Indianapolis, Ind.; Kansas City, Mo.; Lancaster, Pa.; Los Angeles, Cal.; Milwaukee, Wis.; Minneapolis–St. Paul, Minn.; Nashville, Tenn.; New York, N.Y.; Orlando, Fla.; Philadelphia, Pa.; Pittsburgh, Pa.; Portland, Maine; St. Louis, Mo.; San Diego, Cal.; San Francisco–Oakland, Cal.; Seattle–Everett, Wash.; Washington, D.C.; and Wichita, Kans.

Estimating regression equation 6.10 by ordinary least squares for the year 1967 yields

$$Zi = +989.33 - 0.00933Pi + 0.00158Di$$
$$\quad\;\, (+3.28) \qquad (-0.54) \qquad\;\; (+0.07)$$

$$\quad\; + 0.39196Ii - 181.14Ri$$
$$\qquad (+4.19) \qquad (-2.20)$$

$$R^2 = 0.46 \qquad \langle R \rangle_{av}^2 = 0.39 \qquad n = 39 \qquad DF = 34$$

$$F = 6.91956 \qquad\qquad\qquad\qquad\qquad\qquad\qquad (6.16)$$

where the terms in parentheses beneath coefficients are signed $t$-values.

In equation 6.16, all four of the estimated coefficients have the hypothesized signs. In addition, two of the estimated coefficients (those for the exogenous variables $Ii$ and $Ri$) are statistically significant at the 0.025 level or better. The $F$-ratio is statistically significant at beyond the 0.05 level. Finally, the $R^2$ is 0.46 and the $\langle R \rangle_{av}^2$ is 0.39, so that the model explains approximately two-fifths of the total variation in the dependent variable for the year 1967.

The ordinary least-squares estimation of regression equation 6.10 for the year 1972 is given by

$$Zi = +1078.44 - 0.00009Pi + 0.22603Di$$
$$\quad\;\, (+2.83) \qquad (-3.13) \qquad\;\; (+3.15)$$

$$+ 0.33426Ii - 187.14Ri$$
$$(+3.53) \quad (-2.20)$$

$$R^2 = 0.62 \qquad \langle R \rangle_{av}^2 = 0.58 \qquad n = 39 \qquad DF = 34$$

$$F = 12.11698 \tag{6.17}$$

where terms in parentheses are $t$-values.

In equation 6.17, all four of the estimated coefficients have the expected signs. In addition, three of the four estimated coefficients (those for the exogenous variables $Pi$, $Di$, and $Ii$) are statistically significant at the 0.01 level, whereas the fourth estimated coefficient (that for the exogenous variable $Ri$) is statistically significant at the 0.025 level. The $F$-ratio is statistically significant at beyond the 0.01 level. The $R^2$ is 0.62 and the $\langle R \rangle_{av}^2$ is 0.58; hence, the model explains roughly three-fifths of the variation in the endogenous variable for the year 1972.

Estimating regression equation 6.10 by ordinary least squares for the year 1975 yields

$$Zi = +1209.13 - 0.00011Pi + 0.37641Di$$
$$(+2.33) \quad (-2.92) \quad (+3.68)$$

$$+ 0.25744Ii - 167.51Ri$$
$$(+3.90) \quad (-1.57)$$

$$R^2 = 0.59 \qquad \langle R \rangle_{av}^2 = 0.53 \qquad n = 39 \qquad DF = 34$$

$$F = 10.98113 \tag{6.18}$$

where terms in parentheses are $t$-values.

In equation 6.18, all four of the estimated coefficients have the hypothesized signs. In addition, three of the four estimated coefficients (those for the exogenous variables $Pi$, $Di$, and $Ii$) are statistically significant at beyond the 0.01 level. Only the coefficient for the exogenous variable $Ri$ fails to be statistically significant at an acceptable level.[3] The $F$-ratio is statistically significant at the 0.01 level. Finally, the $R^2$ is 0.59 and the $\langle R \rangle_{av}^2$ is 0.53, so that the model explains nearly three-fifths of the variation in the housing-cost variable for the year 1975.

For the year 1978, the ordinary least-squares estimate of regression equation 6.10 is given by

$$Zi = +2530.30 - 0.00009Pi + 0.32506Di$$
$$(+2.94) \qquad (-1.66) \qquad (+3.27)$$

$$+ 0.20741Ii - 329.24Ri$$
$$(+1.77) \qquad (-1.87)$$

$$R^2 = 0.44 \qquad \langle R \rangle_{av}^2 = 0.37 \qquad n = 39 \qquad DF = 34$$

$$F = 8.70112 \hspace{6cm} (6.19)$$

where terms in parentheses are $t$-values.

In equation 6.19, all four of the estimated coefficients have the hypothesized signs. In addition, one estimated coefficient (that corresponding to the
exogenous variable $Di$) is statistically significant at beyond the 0.01 level.
The estimated coefficient for the right-to-work-law variable is statistically
significant at approximately the 0.05 level. Moreover, the estimated coefficients corresponding to the population-size and per-capita-income variables
are statistically significant at beyond the 0.10 level. The $R^2$ is 0.44 and the
$\langle R \rangle_{av}^2$ is 0.37; consequently, the model explains roughly two-fifths of the
variation in the endogenous cost-of-housing variable for the year 1978. The
$F$-ratio is statistically significant at the 0.05 level.

For the year 1979, housing-cost data were available for only twenty-four
metropolitan areas (SMSAs): Atlanta, Ga.; Baltimore, Md.; Boston,
Mass.; Buffalo, N.Y.; Chicago, Ill.; Cincinnati, Ohio; Cleveland, Ohio;
Dallas, Tex.; Denver, Col.; Detroit, Mich.; Honolulu, Hawaii; Houston,
Tex.; Kansas City, Mo.; Los Angeles, Cal.; Milwaukee, Wis.; Minne-
apolis–St. Paul, Minn.; New York, N.Y.; Philadelphia, Pa.; Pittsburgh,
Pa.; St. Louis, Mo.; San Diego, Cal.; San Francisco–Oakland, Cal.; Seat-
tle–Everett, Wash.; and Washington, D.C. Naturally, the reduced number
of observations results in a similarly reduced number of degrees of freedom.
Given twenty-four observations and five estimators, it follows that

$$DF = 24 - 5 = 19 \hspace{4cm} (6.20)$$

where $DF$ is the number of degrees of freedom.

For the year 1979, the ordinary least-squares estimate of regression
equation 6.10 is given by the following:

$$Zi = +3847.12 - 0.00011Pi + 0.34361Di$$
$$(+3.27) \qquad (-1.46) \qquad (+2.79)$$

$$+ \ 0.08331 Ii \ - \ 655.34 Ri$$
$$(+0.68) \qquad (-2.52)$$

$$R^2 = 0.52 \qquad \langle R \rangle_{av}^2 = 0.42 \qquad n = 24 \qquad DF = 19$$

$$F = 8.95917 \tag{6.21}$$

where the terms in parentheses are $t$-values.

In equation estimate 6.21, all four of the estimated coefficients have the expected signs. In addition, two of the four estimated coefficients (those corresponding to the exogenous variables $Di$ and $Ri$) are statistically significant at the 0.01 level. In contrast, the estimated coefficients corresponding to the variables $Pi$ and $Ii$ both fail to be statistically significant at even the 0.10 level. The $R^2$ is 0.52 and the $\langle R \rangle_{av}^2$ is 0.42, so that the model explains approximately one-half of the variation in the cost-of-housing variable for the year 1979. The $F$-ratio is statistically significant at roughly the 0.05 level.

Regression equation 6.10 has been estimated by ordinary least squares for 1967, 1972, 1975, 1978, and 1979. All of the estimations have been cross-sectional in nature, and a total of twenty regression coefficients have been empirically estimated.

The population-size variable exhibited the hypothesized sign in all five of the estimations. However, the estimated coefficient of the variable for population size was statistically significant at an acceptable level in only two of the five regressions. Therefore, only relatively weak empirical support has been generated for the hypothesis that housing costs are a decreasing function of population size. Accordingly, it may well be that

$$\partial Zi / \partial Pi \cong 0. \tag{6.22}$$

Of course, the tentative conclusion expressed in equation 6.22 does not apply to the *overall* level of the cost of living in metropolitan areas.

The population-density variable exhibited the expected positive sign in all five regression estimates. In addition, the estimated coefficient of the population-density variable is statistically significant at acceptable levels in four of the five regression equations. Only for the year 1967 did this variable fail to be statistically significant at an acceptable level. Reasonably strong empirical support has been generated for the hypothesis that housing-cost levels are an increasing function of population density.

The coefficients of the per-capita income variable have the hypothesized signs in all five regression equations. In addition, the estimated coefficient for the per-capita-income variable is statistically significant at the 0.05

level or better in three regressions; furthermore, the coefficient of the income variable is statistically significant at beyond the 0.10 level in a fourth regression equation. Consequently, moderately strong empirical support has been generated for the hypothesis that housing costs are a direct function of per-capita income levels.

Finally, the coefficient of the right-to-work-law variable exhibited the hypothesized negative sign in all five of the regression estimates. In addition, the estimated coefficient of the right-to-work-law variable was statistically significant at an acceptable level in four of the five estimated equations. The coefficient of variable $Ri$ failed to be statistically significant at an acceptable level in only one case, that corresponding to the year 1975. Relatively strong empirical support has been generated for the hypothesis that housing costs are a decreasing function of the presence of right-to-work legislation.

Thus, the empirical results show that the cost of housing is an increasing function of population density and per-capita income, and a decreasing function of right-to-work legislation.

## A Summary of the Empirical Findings

This book has been concerned most fundamentally with the determinants of geographic living-cost differentials among metropolitan areas (SMSAs) in the United States. The first chapter indicated the extent (both in absolute dollars and in relative terms) of geographic living-cost differentials. It also provided indications of the potential economic and public-policy implications of large geographic living-cost differentials. The remainder of the book has been devoted to explaining the determinants of these differentials.

Chapter 2 provided four basic sets of hypotheses to account for the existence of large geographic living-cost differentials. It was argued that living costs are determined, at least in part, by the following four factors or variables: population size, population density, per-capita income levels, and right-to-work legislation. It was argued that, all else held the same (ceteris paribus), the overall cost of living in metropolitan areas is a decreasing function of population size. It was argued that, following Isard (1956) and Nourse (1968), *agglomeration economies* associated with a larger population act to reduce production costs and hence reduce output prices and the overall cost of living. It was also argued that, ceteris paribus, the overall cost of living in a metropolitan area is an increasing function of population density. With increased population density, *transfer diseconomies* raise production costs and hence commodity prices. Next, it was argued that, ceteris paribus, the overall cost of living in a metropolitan area is an increasing function of the per-capita income level. As per-capita income rises, so too does the overall demand for goods and services. Forces of excess demand then act to elevate commodity prices. Finally, it was argued that, ceteris paribus, the overall cost of living in a metropolitan area is a decreasing function of the presence of right-to-work laws. It was argued that the existence of right-to-work laws in an area creates a labor-market environment in which labor costs (the *wage package*) are lower than would be the case in the absence of such laws. The lower labor costs resulting from right-to-work legislation in turn lead to a lower overall commodity-price structure.

Chapter 3 empirically examined the four sets of hypotheses developed in chapter 2. The primary analysis in chapter 3 involved ordinary least-squares estimations of a linear-regression equation for each of the fourteen years from 1966 through 1979. Sufficient data were available to permit an analysis of as many as thirty-nine SMSAs. A total of fifty-six regression coefficients were empirically estimated. In all fifty-six cases, the estimated coefficients of the exogenous variables had the hypothesized signs.

The variables for population size, population density, per-capita income, and right-to-work laws generally performed very well, and the basic hypotheses developed in chapter 2 received extremely strong empirical support. Thus, the overall cost of living in metropolitan areas is a decreasing function of population size and the presence of right-to-work laws. In addition, the overall cost of living in metropolitan areas is an increasing function of population density and the level of per-capita income.

In chapter 4, the basic model examined in chapters 2 and 3 was extended in a number of ways. The first and perhaps the most promising of these extensions takes the following form:

$$Ci = Ci\ (Pi,\ Di,\ Ii,\ Ri,\ Ai) \qquad\qquad (6.23)$$

where $Ci$, $Pi$, $Di$, $Ii$, and $Ri$ are as earlier indicated and $Ai$ is the average unit price of residential heating gas in SMSA $i$.[4]

The exogenous variable $Ai$ is clearly a surrogate for average utility (and fuel) prices in area $i$. Linear-regression equations based on the model in equation 6.23 were estimated by ordinary least squares for all of the years from 1967 through 1975. In all nine cases, the estimated linear coefficient of the variable $Ai$ had the hypothesized positive sign. In addition, in four of the nine cases,[5] the coefficient of variable $Ai$ was statistically significant at beyond the 0.05 level. Hence, in a number of the regressions, the addition of the variable $Ai$ represented a potentially productive extension of the basic system of chapters 2 and 3.

Chapter 4 also investigated the potential impact of property taxation on living costs. It was hypothesized that, for a number of reasons, higher property-tax levels would lead to a higher overall level of the cost of living.[6] The model examined is given by

$$Ci = Ci\ (Pi,\ Di,\ Ii,\ Ri,\ Ti) \qquad (6.24)$$

where $Ci$, $Pi$, $Di$, $Ii$, and $Ri$ are as earlier indicated and $Ti$ is the per-capita property-tax level in SMSA $i$.

Linear regression equations based on the model in equation 6.24 were estimated for the years 1974, 1975, and 1978. In all three cases, the property-tax variable failed to be statistically significant at even the 0.15 level. Hence, it was reasonably concluded that property taxation does *not* significantly effect the overall cost of living.

The basic model was also extended in chapter 4 by using the unionization rate as a replacement for the right-to-work-law dummy variable. The model examined takes the following form:

$$Ci = Ci\ (Pi,\ Di,\ Ii,\ Ui) \qquad (6.25)$$

where $Ci$, $Pi$, $Di$, $Ii$ are as earlier indicated and $Ui$ is the unionization rate in SMSA $i$, expressed as the percentage of the civilian labor force in SMSA $i$ that is unionized.

Linear regressions based on the model impounded in equation 6.25 were estimated by ordinary least squares for the years 1970 and 1978. In both cases, the estimated coefficient of the exogenous variable $Ui$ failed to be statistically significant at even the 0.20 level. Thus, the model expressed in equation 6.25 proved to be inferior to that developed in chapters 2 and 3.

A very simple dynamic model, whose purpose is to identify the determinants of geographic inflation-rate differentials among metropolitan areas, was developed in chapter 5. It was argued that geographic inflation-rate differentials are determined in part by

1. the net in-migration rate;
2. the growth rate of per-capita income;
3. the growth rate of the unionization rate of the civilian labor force; and
4. the growth rate of per-capita state plus local taxation levels.

The empirical analysis of these hypotheses dealt with thirty-six SMSAs over the 1970–1978 time period. A linear-regression model was estimated by ordinary least squares. All four of the estimated coefficients exhibited the hypothesized signs. In addition, three of the four estimated coefficients were statistically significant at the 0.01 level. Overall, then, the model shed useful light on the factors that influence the rate of change over time of the overall cost of living in metropolitan areas.

Finally, this chapter has examined the determinants of the cost of *housing* in metropolitan areas, as opposed to the investigation of the determinants of the *overall* cost of living in metropolitan areas in earlier chapters. A linear-regression model was estimated by ordinary least squares for 1967, 1972, 1975, 1978, and 1979. It was found that the cost of housing is an increasing function of population density and per-capita income levels and a decreasing function of the presence of right-to-work legislation. Thus, with the apparent exception of the population-size variable, the model developed in chapters 2 and 3 provides a useful explanation of the determinants of geographic housing-cost differentials in the United States.

## Limitations and Alternatives

This book has sought to identify and quantify the principal determinants of geographic living-cost levels and geographic living-cost differentials in the United States. To this end, several models have been hypothesized, and a considerable number of empirical estimates have been undertaken. Nevertheless, there are a number of limitations to this study.

The first limitation is that of the data. As noted in chapter 3, there are several potentially important problems with the living-cost data. For example, the geographic living-cost data examined in this book are presumably comparable because of the general similarity of market baskets of household commodities among regions. The degree of geographic comparability of living-cost data is somewhat questionable, however. For instance, the living-costdata reflect differentials in living-cost levels only for established (current) residents. How relevant the living-cost data are for *new* (or potential) residents remains to be seen. In addition, it is not clear that the living-cost data adequately control for geographic differentials in household preferences. It is also unclear whether the living-cost data control adequately for geographic differentials in the quality of commodities and the available mix of commodities.

At another level, it is not entirely clear that the use of the average annual cost of living for a four-person family living on an *intermediate* budget is necessarily the best choice for a living-cost measure. There are several alternative measures of the cost of living that could have been used. For example, in lieu of the intermediate budget, the budget for a low living standard or the budget for a high living standard could have been used. Conceivably, even the budget for a retired couple could have been used. Despite the existence of these various alternatives, however, the use of the intermediate budget may be the most defensible and reasonable because the intermediate budget may well be the budget to which the average (typical) household can most closely relate. Of course, given the high degree of statistical correlation among these various budget alternatives, the choice of a living-cost measure may be an issue of relatively minor importance.

The use of data that measure only the *overall* cost of living also can be questioned. In fact, a housing-costs variable was substituted for the overall-living-cost variable in this chapter. There are several other alternatives to the overall living-cost data as well. For instance, the U.S. Bureau of Labor Statistics data on transportation costs for a four-person family could have been used. Alternatively, the Bureau of Labor Statistics also compiles data for a broad category of living costs known as "other" living costs. These other costs are an interesting amalgam that includes clothing, medical care, gifts, personal care, charitable contributions, basic life insurance, social-security contributions, personal income taxes, and occupational expenses. Or the food costs (budget) that the Bureau of Labor Statistics compiles could be used. Finally, a series of living-cost data consisting of selected components of the overall cost of living could be constructed. For example, housing costs and food costs for each metropolitan area could easily be combined. Clearly, there are a number of different ways in which to measure living costs; the analysis obviously need not be restricted to the overall level of living costs.

The basic models developed in this book could be altered in a number of ways. One of these many possible alterations is given by the following:

$$HPi = f\ (Pi,\ Di,\ Ii,\ Ri) \qquad (6.26)$$

where $HPi$ is the median price of a *new* one-family house in SMSA $i$ in 1978[7] and $Pi$, $Di$, $Ii$, and $Ri$ are as earlier indicated,[8] for 1978.

Expressed in linear form, equation 6.26 becomes:

$$HPi = c_0 + c_1 Pi + c_2 Di + c_3 Ii + c_4 Ri + c_5 \qquad (6.27)$$

where $c_0$ is a constant term and $c_5$ is a stochastic-error term.

Estimating regression equation 6.27 by ordinary least squares generated four coefficients, all of which failed to be statistically significant at even the 0.15 level.

Given the very poor performance of the model expressed in equation 6.26, an alternative model was sought to help explain the new endogenous variable $HPi$. The model finally took the following form:

$$HPi = g\ (Ii,\ Ri,\ EDi) \qquad (6.28)$$

where $HPi$, $Ii$, and $Ri$ are as in equation 6.26, and $EDi$ is the per-capita public-education expenditure level in SMSA $i$ in 1978.[9]

The inclusion of the variable $EDi$ to help explain housing prices is, in effect, an empirical test of the well-known Tiebout hypothesis (Tiebout 1956).[10]
The linear form of equation 6.28 is given by

$$HPi = d_0 + d_1Ii + d_2Ri + d_3EDi + d_4 \qquad (6.29)$$

where $d_0$ is a constant term and $d_4$ is a stochastic-error term.[11]

Estimating regression equation 6.29 by ordinary least squares yields

$$HPi = -10107.02 + 1.41603Ii$$
$$(-0.65) \qquad (+0.89)$$

$$+ 843.02Ri + 114.00EDi$$
$$(+0.27) \qquad (+3.57)$$

$$R^2 = 0.67 \qquad \langle R \rangle_{av}^2 = 0.59 \qquad n = 16 \qquad DF = 12$$

$$F = 2.98761 \qquad\qquad\qquad\qquad (6.30)$$

where terms in parentheses are $t$-values.[12]

The empirical results shown in regression equation 6.30 lend statistical support to the Tiebout hypothesis. In fact, these results are entirely compatible with the earlier findings in Oates (1969). Nevertheless, there is no readily apparent way in which to integrate the model expressed in equations 6.28 through 6.30 into the remainder of this study.
Other modified specifications of the systems developed in this book may potentially provide more utility than the system shown in equations 6.28 through 6.30. For example, the basic model from chapters 2 and 3 might be expanded as follows:

$$Ci = Ci\ (Pi,\ Di,\ Ii,\ Ri,\ ELDi) \qquad (6.31)$$

where $ELDi$ is the percentage of the total population in SMSA $i$ that is elderly.

Presumably, the greater the percentage of the population that is elderly, the greater the degree to which the economy in a metropolitan area tends to be service-oriented. Since a service orientation is less likely than a goods orientation to be subject to (conducive to) scale economies in production, it may reasonably be argued that

$$\partial C_i/\partial ELD_i > 0. \tag{6.32}$$

Alternatively, the basic model from chapters 2 and 3 might be expanded to

$$C_i = C_i \,(P_i, \, D_i, \, I_i, \, R_i, \, MFG_i) \tag{6.33}$$

where $MFG_i$ is the ratio of manufacturing employment in SMSA $i$ to total nonagricultural employment in SMSA $i$.

As the ratio of manufacturing employment to total nonagricultural employment rises, the proportion of an area's economic activity that is subject to scale economies also tends to rise. Consequently, it may logically be argued that

$$\partial C_i/\partial MFG_i < 0. \tag{6.34}$$

It is analytically possible to combine the models in equations 6.31 and 6.33. The resulting model would take the following general form:

$$C_i = h \,(P_i, \, D_i, \, I_i, \, R_i, \, ELD_i, \, MFG_i) \tag{6.35}$$

where it is hypothesized that

$$\partial h/\partial ELD_i > 0 \tag{6.36}$$

and

$$\partial h/\partial MFG_i < 0. \tag{6.37}$$

Because of the possible negative-correlation problem between the variables $ELD_i$ and $MFG_i$, the models in equations 6.31 and 6.33 may be preferable to the model in equation 6.35. Nevertheless, the choice among systems 6.31, 6.33, and 6.35 is ultimately an empirical one.

Finally, there is the issue of whether to adopt single-equation models or multiequation models. All of the models developed in this book and all of the regressions estimated are fundamentally single-equation in nature. It may be, however, that the basic relationships examined here require simultaneous-equation analysis. It may well be that two- or three-equation systems would yield greater insights than would single-equation systems.

An example of a very plausible multiequation system to deal with overall geographic living-cost levels is shown by equations 6.38 and 6.39:

$$Ci = Ci \ (Pi, \ Di, \ Ii, \ Ri) \tag{6.38}$$

$$Ii = Ii \ (Ci, \ . \ . \ .). \tag{6.39}$$

A similar framework for analyzing housing costs is given by the following two-equation system:

$$Zi = Zi \ (Pi, \ Di, \ Ii, \ Ri) \tag{6.40}$$

$$Ii = Ii \ (Zi, \ . \ . \ .). \tag{6.41}$$

Such systems would be expressed in regression-equation form and then estimated by two-stage least squares (2SLS).

A simultaneous-equation specification to deal with regional inflation might also be useful. Consider, for example, the following two-equation system:

$$\Delta Ci = \Delta Ci \ (Mi, \ . \ . \ .) \tag{6.42}$$

$$Mi = Mi \ (\Delta Ci, \ . \ . \ .) \tag{6.43}$$

where $\Delta Ci$ is a measure of the rate of change of the cost of living in area $i$ and $Mi$ is the net in-migration rate to area $i$.

The system shown in equations 6.42 and 6.43 would first be expressed in regression form and then empirically estimated by the 2SLS method.

In summary, then, the data used in this study have a number of potentially troublesome limitations.[13] There are many possible specifications of models other than those examined in this study. The findings generated in this study should not be considered as definitive; to be sure, more work remains to be done.

## Economic and Public-Policy Implications

This book has examined geographic living-cost differentials in the United States. Such differentials have been found to be both large (in dollar terms and in relative terms) and persistent over time (in dollar terms and in relative terms), and they have significant economic and public-policy implications.

In the United States, internal migration has become the principal *short-run* determinant of changes in population distribution and one of the principal *long-run* determinants of changes in population distribution (see West, Hamilton, and Loomis 1976, and Cebula 1979). A number of recent empirical studies, including Renas and Kumar (1978, 1979, and 1981) and Cebula (1979), have found that geographic living-cost differentials have a significant impact on internal migration patterns.[14] Since these geographic living-cost differentials are not only large but persistent, it follows that geographic living-cost differentials have come to profoundly influence both short-run and long-run changes in the population distribution of the United States. It also follows that large and persistent geographic living-cost differentials profoundly influence the functioning of regional labor markets in the United States.

By influencing regional labor markets, geographic living-cost differentials influence: 1) the level and growth-rate pattern of money-wage rates; 2) the level and trend over time of real-wage rates; and 3) the patterns of regional employment levels and of regional employment trends. Indeed, it can even by shown that geographic living-cost differentials can account for the long-observed pattern of persistent money-wage-rate differentials among the various economic regions of the United States.[15]

To illustrate some of the basic impacts of large and persistent geographic living-cost differentials on labor markets, we refer to panels **(a)** and **(b)** of figure 6–1. In panel **(a)** of the diagram, the labor market for region A is represented, whereas in panel **(b)**, the labor market for region B is represented. For simplicity, it is assumed that the economy consists of only these two regions. It is also assumed that the labor units in both regions are economically rational; therefore, the labor units in both regions are entirely free of money illusion. Moreover, it is also assumed that the labor units in both regions are a homogeneous input.

Let us begin the analysis of an interregional labor-market equilibrium in figure 6–1 at money-wage-rate level $W_1$. Thus, the labor market in region A clears at a money-wage rate of $W_1$ and an unemployment level of $L_1$ units, whereas the labor market in region B clears at a money-wage rate of $W_1$ and an employment level of $L'$ units. Let us also recognize the existence of a living-cost differential between these two regions. Specifically, let us assume that the cost of living is higher in region B than in region A. Given that labor units are rational, it follows that labor units will not migrate from region A to region B unless the money-wage rate in region B is sufficiently higher than that in region A to at least compensate for the living-cost differential between the two regions. Let us assume that the money-wage-rate differen-

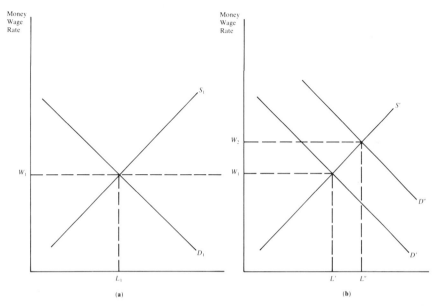

**Figure 6–1.** Interregional Labor-Market Equilibrium

tial necessary to elicit migration from region A to region B must exceed the hourly dollar amount $\alpha$, where $\alpha > 0$.

A necessary condition for net positive migration from region A to region B is the following:

$$W_B - W_A > 0. \tag{6.44}$$

Ignoring moving costs, it follows that the necessary and sufficient condition for net positive migration from region A to region B is given by

$$W_B - W_A > \alpha > 0. \tag{6.45}$$

Observe that the gross migration rate from region A to region B will be zero so long as

$$0 < (W_B - W_A) \leqq \alpha. \tag{6.46}$$

The implications of equations 6.44 through 6.46 can now be illustrated with the aid of figure 6–1. Consider, for example, a rise in the labor-demand schedule in region B from $D'$ to $D''$. The equilibrium money-wage rate in region B rises from $W_1$ to $W_2$ in response to excess labor-demand conditions. The money-wage-rate differential between regions B and A is now given by

$$W_B - W_A = W_2 - W_1 > 0, \qquad (6.47)$$

unless, however, it is also true that

$$W_2 - W_1 > \alpha > 0. \qquad (6.48)$$

Then no gross migration from region A to region B will occur.

For simplicity, let us for the moment assume that, in figure 6–1, the following obtains:

$$W_2 - W_1 = \alpha > 0. \qquad (6.49)$$

If the condition in equation 6.49 holds, then an interregional money-wage-rate differential equal to $\alpha$ dollars per hour exists *in equilibrium*. Moreover, given the living-cost differential between regions A and B, the interregional money-wage-rate differential ($\alpha$) can persist over time. The money-wage-rate differential also can persist over time so long as the following condition obtains:

$$0 < W_2 - W_1 < \alpha \qquad (6.50)$$

The condition in inequality 6.49 is tolerable since it implies equality of *real-wage* rates between regions. However, the condition in inequality 6.50 is of greater concern since interregional money-wage-rate differentials are accompanied by interregional *real-wage-rate* differentials. Since the condition in inequality 6.49 is obviously a special case, it can be reasonably inferred that large and persistent geographic living-cost differentials produce not only interregional *money-wage-rate* differentials but also interregional *real-wage-rate* differentials.

Of course, by influencing the geographic distribution of human resources, geographic living-cost differentials also influence the pattern of regional economic-growth rates. This can even be inferred from figure 6–1. In fact, as noted by Cebula (1979), since the most geographically mobile members of society tend to be those persons who possess the greatest relative endowments of human capital, living-cost differentials could significantly contribute over time to a pattern of increasingly divergent regional economic-growth rates in the United States.

The fact that living-cost differentials influence geographic mobility also generates many public-policy implications. For example, as an area with relatively low living costs attracts new migrants, it will experience a rising demand for local public goods and services such as schools, teachers, drainage and sewage systems, police and fire protection, and roads. The low-living-cost area in question will also very likely experience the need for additional revenue and for new issues of tax-free bonds to help finance capital improvements and expansion. These issues of tax-free bonds obviously will affect credit markets, with the final effect of upward pressure on interest rates (especially long-term interest rates) and a diminished availability of credit to the private sector of the economy.

Areas with relatively high living costs, in contrast, are likely (on balance) to lose population and industry and to potentially be faced with a declining tax base and an unwanted excess capacity in the utilization of public capital. Ironically, areas with high living costs may also then be forced to resort to the credit markets for needed funds.[16] Given the massive federal budget deficits being generated during the early- and mid-1980s, the predicted pattern of increased local-government activity in the credit markets leads to a rather dismal prospect for achieving substantially lower interest rates in the coming years. The prospects for adverse economic conditions in the foreseeable future abound!

## Notes

1. It follows from equation 6.2 that $Rit = 0$ or $Rit = 1$.

2. Once again, because of the presence of a dummy variable $(0, 1)$ in the regression format, a linear specification is necessary.

3. As noted in earlier chapters, the minium acceptable level of statistical significance is the 0.05 level, that is, the 0.95 confidence level.

4. See equation 6.1.

5. These four cases correspond to the years 1971, 1973, 1974, and 1975.

6. Related to this argument, see Cebula (1974, p. 877).

7. The variable $HPi$ is measured in current dollars, as was the case for both the variables $Ci$ and $Zi$.

8. See equation 6.1.

9. These figures include all federal, state, and local government outlays for public education.

10. Related to the Tiebout hypothesis, see also the studies by Cebula (1978), Buchanan (1968), Oates (1969), Hamilton (1976), and Edel and Sclar (1974).

11. The sixteen SMSAs examined in regression equations 6.29 and 6.30 are Atlanta, Ga.; Chicago, Ill.; Dallas, Tex.; Dayton, Ohio; Denver, Col.; Houston, Tex.; Kansas City, Mo.; Los Angeles, Cal.; Minneapolis–St.

Paul, Minn.; Nashville, Tenn.; Orlando, Fla.; Philadelphia, Pa.; St. Louis, Mo.; San Diego, Cal.; San Francisco–Oakland, Cal.; and Seattle–Everett, Wash. These metropolitan areas were all examined in chapters 2 through 4.

12. The year 1978 was chosen entirely at random. It might be noted, however, that running the regression for several other years has generated the same general patterns of findings.

13. There are potentially, of course, more limitations to the analysis. Consider, for example, the per-capita-income variable. Are there potentially more appropriate variables that could have been used in the analysis instead of per-capita income? Arguments can be made for the use of the money-wage rate (in manufacturing) or for the use of median income. Related to the use of the latter variable, see Graves (1976), and Cebula (1979).

14. Related to the issue at hand, see also Alperovich (1979), and Kirk (1982).

15. Related to these observed money-wage-rate differentials, see Scully (1969 and 1971), and Buckley (1979).

16. These credit demands by high-living-cost areas are likely to be manifested principally in the shorter-term bond markets.

## References

Alperovich, G. 1979. "The Cost of Living, Labor Market Opportunities, and the Migration Decision: A Case of Misspecification?: Comment." *Annals of Regional Science* 13:102–105.
Buchanan, J.M. 1968. *The Demand and Supply of Public Goods*. Pacific Palisades, Cal.: Rand-McNally.
Buckley, J.E. 1979. "Do Area Wages Reflect Area Living Costs?" *Monthly Labor Review* 102:24–30.
———. 1974. "Interstate Migration and the Tiebout Hypothesis: An Analysis According to Race, Sex, and Age." *Journal of the American Statistical Association* 69:876–879.
———. 1978. "An Empirical Note on the Tiebout-Tullock Hypothesis." *Quarterly Journal of Economics* 93:705–711.
Cebula, R.J. 1979. *The Determinants of Human Migration*. Lexington, Mass.: D.C. Heath, Lexington Books.
Edel, M., and Sclar, E. 1974. "Taxes, Spending, and Property Values: Supply Adjustment in a Tiebout-Oates Model." *Journal of Political Economy* 82:941–955.
Graves, P.E. 1976. "A Reexamination of Migration, Economic Opportunity, and the Quality of Life." *Journal of Regional Science* 16:107–112.
Hamilton, B.W. 1976. "Capitalization of Intrajurisdictional Differences in Local Tax Prices." *American Economic Review* 66:743–753.

Isard, W., 1956. *Location and Space Economy*. Cambridge, Mass.: MIT Press.

Kirk, R.J. 1982. "Differentials in the Cost of Living." *Growth and Change* 13:24–30.

Nourse, H. 1968. *Regional Economics*. New York: McGraw-Hill.

Oates, W.E. 1969. "The Effects of Property Taxes and Local Spending on Property Values: An Empirical Study of Tax Capitalization and the Tiebout Hypothesis." *Journal of Political Economy* 77:957–971.

Renas, S.M., and Kumar, R. 1978. "The Cost of Living, Labor Market Opportunities, and the Migration Decision: A Case of Misspecification?" *Annals of Regional Science* 12:95–104.

———. 1979. "The Cost of Living, Labor Market Opportunities, and the Migration Decision: A Case of Misspecification?: Reply." *Annals of Regional Science* 13:106–108.

———. 1981. "The Cost of Living, Labor Market Opportunities, and the Migration Decision: Some Additional Evidence." *Annals of Regional Science* 15:74–79.

Scully, G.W. 1969. "Interstate Wage Differentials: A Cross-Sectional Analysis." *American Economic Review* 59:757–773.

———. 1971. "The North-South Manufacturing Wage Differential, 1869–1919." *Journal of Regional Science* 11:235–252.

Tiebout, C.M. 1956. "A Pure Theory of Local Expenditures," *Journal of Political Economy* 64:416–424.

West, D.A., Hamilton, J.R., and Loomis, R.A. 1976. "A Conceptual Framework for Guiding Policy-Related Research on Migration." *Land Economics* 52:66–76.

# Index

# About the Author

**Richard J. Cebula** is a professor of economics at Emory University. He received the A.B. from Fordham College, the M.A. from the University of Georgia, and the Ph.D. from Georgia State University. Dr. Cebula has published numerous articles in major journals in the fields of migration, macroeconomics, and microeconomics; he is also the author of *The Determinants of Human Migration* (Lexington Books, 1979). In addition, he has presented papers at meetings of major professional societies in the United States.